PICTORIAL GUIDE
TO
HOUSE PLANTS

by
M. Jane Coleman Helmer, Ph.D.
Karla S. Decker Hodge, B.S., Editor

First Edition 1993
First Printing June 1993

ISBN 0-89484-053-3 Softcover
Library of Congress Card No. 93-078210

 *Merchants Publishing Company*
3500 Sprinkle Road, Kalamazoo, Michigan 49002

Printed in United States of America.

CONTENTS

ACKNOWLEDGEMENTS

The author and editor thank the following companies and individuals for their invaluable assistance in providing information, encouragement, and advice throughout the preparation of this book:

Dr. Edward A. Cope, Assistant Curator, L. H. Bailey Hortorium, Cornell University, Ithaca, NY: *Consultant*

Dr. Louis F. Wilson, retired, U.S.D.A. Forest Service; Professor Emeritus, Michigan State University; Punta Gorda, FL: *Consultant*

Dr. Richard W. Henley, Professor of Environmental Horticulture, Central Florida Research and Education Center, Apopka, FL: *Consultant*

Dr. Robert G. Anderson, Professor of Extension Floriculture, University of Kentucky, Lexington, KY: *Consultant*

Dale Van Eck, Merchants Publishing Company: *Concept, Design*

Dean Clark, Merchants Publishing Company: *Graphic Designer*

Carri Town, Merchants Publishing Company: *Typographer*

Photographs are from Merchants' comprehensive library of horticultural subjects.

INTRODUCTION TO HOUSE PLANTS

Healthy living plants make attractive and welcoming settings for home and business. Their natural forms soften somewhat unchanging surroundings, and a room with house plants or fresh flowers has in it a welcoming ambience. The therapeutic as well as aesthetic properties of plants and flowers are well-known: not only do they enhance a sense of well-being, but caring for and working with living plant materials makes for a satisfying and creative partnership with nature.

When living plants are present, the indoor environment becomes healthier as well as more attractive. Plants add humidity to soften dry air for easier breathing. Plant groups and screens muffle noises and guide traffic. Plants filter dust and soot from the air and, through photosynthesis, reduce its carbon dioxide content while increasing the oxygen. And there is growing evidence that living plants actually clean and purify the air we breathe.

PLANTS FOR SWEETER AIR

Indoor pollutants can be five to ten times more concentrated than those outside. Energy-efficient homes and offices are designed and built to permit little if any unwanted ventilation. Planned air movement usually recirculates the air within a building or room, for comfort and uniform temperature distribution. 'Fresh' air may simply be cooler or deodorized. Many construction materials, furnishings, and tobacco smoke add air-borne pollutants such as formaldehyde, benzene, trichloroethylene, and scores of other chemicals.

The *Foliage for Clean Air Council* has documented living plants' ability to absorb these chemicals. All plants tested have some air-purifying qualities, and some of them can remove as much as 85 percent of certain common pollutants. The most effective indoor plants include aglaonemas, azaleas, bromeliads, dieffenbachias, dracaenas, English ivy, pot mums, palms, and various epiphytes.

As few as one efficient plant for every one hundred square feet can make a healthy difference to indoor air quality. The plant with its soil or growing medium and associated microorganisms — the whole living system — has been shown to be a more effective and lasting filter than fresh-cut flowers and foliage or soil alone.

TODAY'S HOUSE PLANTS

Many of today's indoor plants have been bred and selected in recent years. Their development complements advances in architecture and lighting that have improved both living and working environments. Better indoor environments mean better conditions for plants.

A wide selection of foliage and flowering plants is available for every indoor situation. Some plants survive dimly lighted corners, while others flourish in bright sunny windows. There are plants for growing in water as well as those that tolerate dry atmospheres. Artificial lighting assures plant health as it supplements or replaces natural illumination. Sizes range from tiny dish garden plants to large specimen trees for interior landscapes. Indoor plants can be grown as single specimens or grouped in planters, jardinieres and window boxes; as trees or in hanging baskets; and in semi-closed containers like brandy-snifters, bottles and terrariums.

Foliage plants

Foliage plants are often relatively permanent features, being the trees, shrubs, and ground covers of the interior scene. A single weeping fig *(Ficus benjamina)* or basket of grape ivy *(Cissus rhombifolia)* can become a focal point; a group of plants might include those that differ in height, leaf form, and color. Feathery palms and cascading or upright ferns lighten massive, solid color settings; and the larger-leaved philodendrons add visual strength to rooms that are decorated either with continuous color or with small and varied patterns.

With the added seasonal displays of, say, hydrangea and annual flowering plants like calceolaria and cineraria *(Senecio Xhybridus)*, the indoor plant scene can easily be varied. Other flowering plants like many begonias, bromeliads, some gesneriads, anthurium and the peace lily *(Spathiphyllum)* serve a two-fold decorative purpose. They provide the brilliance of color in season, and when flowers have faded they are attractive foliage plants that need not be removed from view.

Flowering plants

Flowering plants assure indoor color throughout the year. Winter-flowering begonias and bromeliads like billbergia are followed closely by the cyclamen, Christ-thorn *(Euphorbia Xkeysii)* and zygocactus *(Schlumbergera)*. Lengthening days bring forth blossoms in the goldfish plant *(Columnea)*, firecracker flower *(Crossandra)*, and many cacti. And in late spring more of the gesneriads come into flower: the lipstick vines *(Aeschynanthus)*, miniature sinnningias, and episcia. Summer is the time for profuse geraniums *(Pelargonium)*, fuchsias, and miniature roses. And, as days become shorter, flowers appear on the wax plants *(Hoya)* and long-lived bromeliads like aechmea and neoregelia; early blossoms appear on the Thanksgiving cactus *(Schlumbergera)*. To complete the year, color is continued through winter with kalanchoe and poinsettia *(Euphorbia pulcherrima)*.

For plants that become dormant or need different treatment when flowers have faded, after-flowering information is included with care details in this book. Examples are the holiday plants like poinsettia *(Euphorbia pulcherrima)*, azalea *(Rhododendron)*, Christmas kalanchoe *(K. blossfeldiana)*, Christmas cherry *(Solanum pseudo-capsicum)*, Easter lily *(Lilium)*; flowering plants like tuberous begonia, pot mum *(Chrysanthemum)*, cyclamen, geranium *(Pelargonium)*, gloxinia *(Sinningia)*, hydrangea, miniature rose *(Rosa)*; short-term indoor plants like caladium, calceolaria, cineraria *(Senecio Xhybridus)*, impatiens, rose periwinkle *(Catharanthus roseus)*, primrose *(Primula)*; and bulb flowers such as amaryllis *(Hippeastrum)*, hyacinth *(Hyacinthus)*, and tulip *(Tulipa)*.

Hanging plants

A number of indoor plants — both foliage and flowering — make ideal and attractive hanging displays. These include natural trailers like English ivy *(Hedera)*, lipstick vine *(Aeschynanthus)*, and wax plant *(Hoya)*: cascading ferns and spider plants *(Chlorophytum)*; and some with upright-to-spreading habits such as prayer plant *(Maranta)*.

The shade loving ivies, purple waffle plant *(Hemigraphis* 'Exotica')*, and trailing philodendrons brighten dull corners and hallways. Brightly lighted spots are great for strawberry begonia *(Saxifraga sarmentosa)*, English ivy *(Hedera helix)*, and many others. And seasonal flowering plants like ivy geranium *(Pelargonium peltatum)* and busy Lizzie *(Impatiens)* enjoy sunny positions indoors.

Plants that hang not only leave tables and countertops uncluttered, but are safely out of the reach of children and pets. And where space is limited, hanging gardens may be the only way to use plants.

Life span of house plants

All living plants have useful lives that vary from a few months to many years. With regular attention and the absence of serious problems, plants in a mixed indoor group can be replaced one by one rather than all at once — each time bringing a fresh look to the display.

A number of indoor plants, comfortable in their settings, thrive for a long time with adequate care. Many, like aglaonema and spathiphyllum with moderate to low light needs, tolerate a range of indoor climates. These, as well as the slow-growing and even more tolerant sansevieria and cast-iron plant *(Aspidistra elatior)*, are among the longest lived. Larger plants like the palms, weeping fig *(Ficus benjamina)*, bird-of-Paradise *(Strelitzia)*, and Norfolk Island pine *(Araucaria heterophylla)* will grow for many years in good conditions. They may even outgrow their space.

Other indoor plants have relatively short useful and decorative lifespans. Fast-growing vines like nephthytis *(Syngonium)*, Swedish ivy *(Plectranthus)*, and wandering Jew *(Zebrina pendula)* can become overgrown or spindly within a few years. They often provide plenty of material for propagation (page 12), and replacement plants can be home-grown. Vigorously growing African violets *(Saintpaulia)* and ferns need periodic division to prevent weakened growth. Taller plants like dumb cane *(Dieffenbachia)* and zebra plant *(Aphelandra)* become 'leggy' as lower leaves are lost.

A BALANCED ENVIRONMENT

All living plants need light, warmth, water, and nutrients for continued life and growth. While each of the necessary factors is discussed separately, it is their balance that affects the total well-being of plants. For instance, when temperatures are reduced, growth slows down or stops; plants survive with less light and need less frequent watering and little or no fertilizing — though they hardly prosper. When one factor changes, aim to adjust the others to maintain a balanced environment.

CARING FOR HOUSE PLANTS

A selection of foliage plants is available for every indoor situation.

Help a new plant to adjust

Any living thing that is transferred to a new environment undergoes a period of adjustment. For the plant this usually means becoming accustomed to the drier atmosphere, warmer climate, and reduced light levels of home or office. Plants offered for indoor use are usually well able to survive and even to thrive in these conditions, even though they may have been produced in quite different environments.

However, the move from one climate to another results in changes to the plants' root-shoot ratio and often to its internal leaf structure. These changes have often begun before the plant is offered for sale, and they continue until the new plant has adjusted — become acclimated — to its final environment.

The air in homes and offices is almost always drier than that in greenhouses and other plant production areas. The relative humidity (RH) in a greenhouse is 70-90%, while in most homes it averages 35-50% for much of the year. In drier climates and during times of artificial heating and cooling, indoor humidity can be much lower. After being moved into a drier place, the plant will most likely lose water rapidly from its upper parts, while its roots — developed to supply water to a less demanding plant — are temporarily unable to replace the transpired water. There simply isn't enough water-absorbing root surface. A new plant tends to wilt, and it may lose a few flowers or mature leaves during the first week or two in its new home.

Leaf drop may result from suddenly reduced light: the plant is unable to sustain all the leaves that developed in its previous location. Usually leaf loss is relatively insignificant. But alarming losses may take place from small-leaved trees, notably the weeping fig *(Ficus benjamina)*. Even a partially conditioned (acclimatized) weeping fig can drop as much as one-fifth of its foliage, and recover fully with new leaves opening on the same branches (some twigs will be lost). However, if leaf loss from a plant continues for several weeks, some other factor should be suspected; see pages 17-19 for more details of plant troubles.

For the first week or two, the plant probably uses extra water; check frequently to be sure the soil doesn't dry so much that the plant wilts, though allow it to dry somewhat between waterings (page 8). Some smaller varieties may be helped temporarily by misting. Even if it is a sun lover, keep the new plant out of direct sunlight while it adjusts. Some leaves may be lost anyway, but new roots soon develop to supply the increased demand for water. If the plant isn't needed for immediate display, and it will tolerate the lower temperature, place it in a cool position (55-60°F, 13-16°C) to help it adjust; leaves and flowers lose less water into cooler air. And for safety's sake, isolate new plants if possible during this time of adjustment until you are sure they don't harbor any pest or disease problems that can be passed to other plants.

CARE OF A NEW PLANT: THE FIRST TWO WEEKS
• Be sure the soil does not dry out at least for the first week or two, so moisture is always available for the roots to supply the increased needs of leaves and flowers. Mist with water (check individual plants for tolerance).
 NOTE: cacti, succulents and bromeliads are exceptions; unless they are flowering, they should be left dry especially if purchased during the fall or winter.
• Move the plant to a cooler place at night to reduce water loss in warm dry air.
• Avoid direct sunlight, even for full sun loving plants; this will keep water loss to a minimum while new roots develop to sustain the flowers and leaves.

Supply basic needs

The light and temperature needs of indoor plants cover a range of conditions without being exacting. Interior landscaping plants in office and other commercial displays are carefully chosen for the ones that are suited to the location. For home decoration, where more individual care can be given, the variety of suitable plants is greater. Different rooms may offer a variety of climates, some with lots of sun and extra warmth, some which are always shaded and cooler, and others where nights are usually well below day temperatures. Make use of these differences in plant selection for each location, and enjoy the natural grace of many different flowering and foliage plants.

Foliage plants are available for a range of conditions.

A sheer curtain between plants and sunlight will help protect tender plant tissue.

LIGHT

Intensity

In home and other indoor environments, light is usually the one factor that limits plant growth. Plants that grow to full-size trees outdoors in their natural environments can be maintained indoors as moderate to large container items. In general, indoor plants tolerate lower-than-natural light levels to the point at which growth stops altogether. Although both duration and intensity can affect flower development, natural daylength is adequate for the maintenance and growth of most indoor plants. Plant growth is usually slower in the shorter days of winter.

The following recommended light levels, together with a balance of all other environmental factors, aim to maintain foliage mass and color, and to sustain the life of open flowers and assist normal development of semi-open blossoms. Tight buds generally open only in brightly lighted situations and may even require full sun.

BRIGHT LIGHT (BL): full sun or bright indirect light
The strongest light — full sun or bright indirect light — comes from a southern exposure, with east and west facing windows providing bright light in the morning and afternoon, respectively. Plants placed in or near sunlit windows, or where there is strong reflected light, will receive bright light. Take care not to expose delicate blossoms to full noonday or afternoon sunshine: petals quickly dry out and wilt.

MODERATE LIGHT (ML): partial shade or diffused light
Partial shade or diffused light generally prevails in an average to well-lighted position out of direct sunshine or with a sheer curtain between plants and sunlight. Plants needing this intensity of light are best placed inside the room 4 to 8 feet (1.2 to 2.4 meters) from the window, or close to one that faces north. These plants often grow well in brighter indirect light.

LOW LIGHT (LL): shade
Low light, or shade, provides just about enough light for comfortable reading. Dim corners and positions more than 8 feet (2.4 meters) from bright windows are suitable for plants that prefer low light. These plants may also tolerate brighter light, though they will require conditioning through gradually increased light intensities over a period of several weeks.

Foliage plants are available for every light regime. Flowering plants in flower usually prefer bright indirect or moderate (diffused) light.

The combination of exposure and distance from windows provides a guide to the different light intensities in a room with one or more windows. An easy hand shadow test can be used for an approximation of light intensity. If natural daylight is to be supplemented or be replaced by artificial light, a more precise measure may be needed. Objective measurement is also needed when the strength of the available light source is in doubt. Specialized light meters provide readings in foot-candles, the units used to describe the intensity of light at a given distance from its source.

HAND SHADOW TEST CHECKS LIGHT INTENSITY
A simple hand shadow test can check the strength of light that will reach indoor plants. With one hand held about 12" (30cm) above a sheet of paper placed on the surface that will hold the plant(s), note the kind of shadow that is cast, and compare it with the following descriptions:

BL - BRIGHT A distinct, sharp shadow is cast by bright indirect light or full sun. This brightest indoor light occurs in or near sunny windows, and in places with strong reflected light.

ML - MODERATE A definite shadow with a fuzzy outline indicates moderate light. This intensity, without direct sunshine, is usually seen 4 to 8 feet (1.2 to 2.4 meters) from a bright window, or close to a north-facing or otherwise sunless window. Plants that need diffused light or partial shade grow well here.

LL - LOW A barely visible shadow with no distinct outline indicates subdued or low light. This is the intensity of light reaching locations more than 8 feet (2.4 meters) from a bright window, in dull corners, in rooms with windows that are blocked from full daylight, and in areas or rooms that are illuminated only with fluorescent lights. Low light or shade tolerant plants will grow in these locations.

Indoor Plants and Artificial Light

Fluorescent or incandescent lighting can be used to supplement natural daylight, or to replace it entirely. For supplemental lighting in small areas, incandescent bulbs or spotlights are fine for short periods. But for longer term installations, more efficient and cooler fluorescent lighting should provide all or most of the illumination. Use supplemental lighting to enhance natural daylight or to lengthen days to maintain active growth. Use artificial light to replace natural, with 12-16 lighted hours each day.

Groups of actively growing plants may need a bright 300-400 foot-candles of light, measured at average plant height. This intensity can be supplied by four 40-watt fluorescent tubes, with reflector, suspended 24" (60cm) above the plants.

Most indoor foliage plants will grow at 100-150 foot candles (moderate to low), and many of them can survive for a year or more with much less light — as low as 50 foot-candles (just enough for reading). Two 40-watt tubes with reflector, suspended 24" (60cm) above the plants, or one 40-watt tube with reflector at 12" (30cm) above the plants, supply 100-150 foot-candles of light. Incandescent light sources can also provide adequate intensities with little danger of scorching the plants, so long as there is some air movement: one 300-watt bulb, with reflector, at a distance of about 48" (120cm), supplies about 100 foot-candles of light.

A combination of cool white and warm white tubes (1:1), or daylight tubes alone, provides a balanced quality of light both for growth and for appearance. Specialized plant lights can also be used with success, though these usually cost more. Since the light output from any lamp or tube falls off with age — meaning plants receive less light from old tubes than from new — they should be replaced at regular intervals. Light from the center of a fluorescent tube is usually more intense than that from the ends; this difference can be used to advantage for plants whose light needs vary.

TEMPERATURE

The temperature ranges given with the individual care instructions on pages 22 through 126 are those within which optimum maintenance or growth and flower life (where applicable) will be achieved. Recommendations are based on two general temperature regimes.

CA - COOL TO AVERAGE temperature plants grow best with days of 60-75°F (16-24°C), while nights may go as low as 45°F (7°C).

WA - AVERAGE TO WARM temperature plants need days of 70-80°F (21-27°C), and they will not be harmed by temperatures as high as 85°F (29°C) in the sun with fresh air. Nights can fall to 60-65°F (16-18°C), even as low as 55°F (13°C) for some varieties.

Indoor plants, especially those grown primarily for their foliage, will often adapt to different environments from those stated. With adequate adjustment of other factors, they can survive at cooler or even slightly warmer temperatures. But for some, temperature tolerance may be more limited than the range of either regime. In both instances, specific temperature need is usually indicated by a statement in the care instructions for the individual plant or group of plants.

Many flowering plants retain their flowers longer at a temperature cooler than 65°C (18°C). For example, pot mum *(Chrysanthemum)*, kalanchoe, calceolaria, cineraria *(Senecio Xhybridus)*, and azalea *(Rhododendron)* are all best with 55-60°F minimum nights (13-16°C). The flowers are of prime importance for these plants, and their longevity will be improved by lower night temperatures than are found in most living rooms. For the best keeping quality, therefore, move such plants to a cooler place at night.

However, some groups like the African violet and other gesneriads (page 16) are better kept in average to warm conditions, with night minimum of 60-65°F (16-18°C); at cooler temperatures these plants will lose flower buds. Bromeliads (page 14) tolerate a broad range of temperatures and their flowers are less fragile than those of other flowering indoor plants.

SOME FACTS ABOUT WINDOWS
Sunlight streaming through a window quickly warms up a room. Direct sun heats any surface it contacts: furnishings can be bleached and plants scorched. While delicate plant tissues, especially flowers and shade-loving foliage plants, are most susceptible, the majority of foliage and flowering house plants prefer some protection from full, scorching midday sun during summer. In winter, direct sun is usually, though not always, less intense.

Cool night temperatures outside tend to make the air just inside windows cool, especially inside single pane windows. In winter this may freeze plants; a temperature of only 40°F (5°C) will chill and damage warmer climate plants, as well as the more tender flowers. Therefore, on winter nights bring plants away from the windows. Aim to avoid extreme temperature fluctuations, for even though most plants thrive with nights 10-15°F cooler than days (a drop of 6-9°C), a rapid change of 30-40°F (16-22°C) in either direction can kill.

RELATIVE HUMIDITY

Even though indoor air is frequently drier than optimum for most plants, all but a few adapt well to the comfortable relative humidity (RH) range of 25 to 50 percent. Both winter heating and summer air-conditioning seasons, when the home is tightly closed, are times during which the indoor RH often drops below comfort level. Most plants are stressed at less than 25% relative humidity. Water is lost faster than it can be replaced. Photosynthesis slows or stops altogether. Bright, fresh foliage becomes dull and bluish even before it wilts. The most common long-term effects of low RH are brown leaf edges, dry leaves, and loss of flowers and buds.

Increase humidity around plants by grouping so they create their own more humid microclimate. Such an arrangement can be useful where artificial lighting is used during winter to maintain active growth. A clear plastic tent or canopy over, but not touching, plants under growing lights will keep moist air around tender cuttings and seedlings. With climate controls or a single room humidifier, air can be maintained at a comfortable 35-45% RH; this level is fine for most plants.

Most ferns and gesneriads (pages 15 and 16) prefer a higher relative humidity of 50% or more. With adequate lighting, the kitchen and bathroom — more humid than the rest of the house — offer ideal conditions for plants that prefer higher humidity levels. At the dry end of the spectrum, many cacti and succulents (page 15) tend to rot if the RH exceeds 30-50%. They thrive in warm living room conditions, and on sunny windowsills.

Plants with special humidity requirements are noted in the descriptions and individual care instructions on pages 22 through 126.

Increase humidity around plants by grouping them close together.

WATERING

The rate at which a plant uses and loses water depends primarily on its rate of growth and how much light it receives. Watering **frequency**— how often it should be watered — depends on the plant's response to these and other factors such as temperature, relative humidity, time of year, air movement, root type, and soil content. A group of different plants in different size containers may have individual ideal watering needs, but in practice and with experience most or all plants in the group can be watered at the same time. Individual plant needs are accommodated through practical compromises.

A good rule of thumb is that underwatering (watering less often) is always better than overwatering. Plants that are too dry will show it with softening foliage that starts to wilt; at this stage it's not too late for them to recover. Overwatered plants may also wilt, but because many roots have already rotted they are often beyond recovery.

All plant roots need oxygen as well as water; this usually comes from air in the soil. Indoor plant soil must be allowed at least to start drying between waterings so fresh air can be drawn into the root zone. In fact, plants can be allowed to dry almost to wilting before water need be given again. Different plants tend to wilt at different soil moisture levels, and the three broad categories for watering frequency accommodate these differences.

MS - MOIST SOIL

Some plants, like ferns that grow in light humusy soil, should not be allowed to dry out at all. Their foliage tends to wilt even as the soil surface dries. These plants can be watered when the soil starts drying, before it gets powder-dry. Soil structure is such that rapid drainage into and through the soil ensures that air is drawn in even while soil particles are saturated.

PD - PARTLY DRY SOIL

Most indoor plants prefer alternating moist and partly dry soils. After a thorough watering, the soil is allowed to become partially dry. The surface becomes thoroughly dry, and often the top inch or two of soil (especially in large containers) is also dry. Although little damage will be done if some of these plants dry to wilting, it is best to water them before the soil becomes dry to the bottom of the pot.

DS - DRY SOIL

Plants such as cacti and succulents thrive when their soil is allowed to dry out completely between waterings. Periods of drought are part of their life cycle, and many of them can be left dry without harm. For example, Christmas cactus *(Schlumbergera bridgesii)* requires a 'hardening' time, after its vigorous spring growth, to stimulate flowering.

Soil moisture content is the chief indicator of watering need. The look and feel of the soil are quick and easy guides; when its surface is dark and damp to the touch, the whole rootball is probably moist — as it should be if it has just been watered. As it dries, the soil becomes paler though it will continue to feel moist for some time. Since the surface usually dries before the rest of the root ball, the "feel" of the soil is a useful indicator and the entire root ball will rarely dry out. Another guide is weight: the whole plant with its soil and container gets lighter as the soil dries; weight is especially useful when checking hanging plants for watering need.

Watering with tap water is fine, though water straight from the cold tap may be too cold for plants. It is best to use water at room temperature: that is, above 60°F (16°C). Either add a little warm water (taking care not to cook the plants) or leave it to stand overnight so the water temperature can adjust to that of the room. The chlorine in many tap water supplies does not usually harm plants, and most will escape when water stands in an open container for 12 to 24 hours.

Chemically softened water is also fine, provided the softening equipment is functioning correctly. This water still contains chemicals, replacing lime with more soluble compounds. Fluorides, however, can harm some indoor plants. Over a period of time, added fluorides may cause brown spots and/or leaf tip burn on varieties of dracaena, cordy-

line, and spider plant *(Chlorophytum)*; similar damage has also been noted in prayer plants *(Maranta)*, calathea, agave and some lilies. For other causes of similar symptoms see pages 17-19.

• WATERING FROM THE TOP is the quickest way to water indoor plants; the space between the soil surface and the rim of the pot acts as a catchment space for water. Fill up the pot as many times as it takes for water to drain out through drainage holes at the bottom of the pot. There may be immediate drainage of water that has simply run through the cracks: when this happens, leave the runoff to be absorbed by the dry soil, and add more at the top after a while; repeat this procedure until the soil is completely re-moistened and excess water remains.

Ideally, any excess water that remains half an hour after watering is discarded. Since this may not be practical, the excess is absorbed by soil and plants. Some soluble chemicals (salts) remain in the soil in concentrations that increase with each watering and fertilization. Plan to leach or flush out these soluble salts at intervals: see next page.

Containers with drainage holes makes watering easy because, when all the soil has been moistened, the excess water simply drains out. With some experience, watering plants in watertight containers can be just as successful, resulting in plants that are every bit as healthy as those grown in pots with drainage holes.

For a plant in a watertight container, tilt the pot to allow the excess to drain out; or use a dipstick.

For soil that has become completely dry and shrunken, immerse the whole pot in a bowl of water for 30 minutes or until bubbles stop rising from the soil; then drain and discard the excess.

• WATERING FROM THE BOTTOM may be preferred for tender-leaved plants like African violets *(Saintpaulia)*, and for those whose top growth totally covers the soil. Either add water to the plant's saucer, and repeat as it is absorbed until no more is taken up; or immerse the pot in water to its rim for 15 to 20 minutes, then let it drain.

WATERING

From the top or the bottom.

Immerse pot in water if soil is too dry; drain after about 30 minutes.

Soluble Salts and Leaching

When plants are fertilized, soluble chemicals are added to the soil. Most waters contain chemicals too, so even when plants are only watered the soluble salt content increases. A growing plant does not, nor does it need to, absorb all the soluble chemicals that accumulate in the soil. Their concentration increases until plant roots are damaged, causing subsequent foliage loss, reduced size of new growth, wilting even while the soil is moist, and collapse of the whole plant.

Good watering practices help to keep the soluble salt build-up to a minimum, if the excess water (really a solution) is discarded every time plants are watered. If this is not practical, and with regular watering and fertilization, the accumulated soluble salts should be flushed out of the soil by leaching at intervals of 2-3 months. Even when the drainage water is discarded each time plants are watered, it's a good practice to leach the soil once or twice a year. Do this when plants are 'spring-cleaned' indoors or out on a calm, warm day, and again before winter so soil can be allowed to dry more between waterings when growth is slower.

• TO LEACH HOUSE PLANTS, water thoroughly several times and discard the drainage solution; or immerse the pots in a bowl of water to saturate the soil, remove after 15 to 30 minutes or when bubbles stop rising, and allow to drain. Containers with no drainage holes should be tilted to let the drainage solution run out over the edge. Repeat this procedure one or more times with clean water, or until the water draining out looks clear.

WATERING IN WINTER

In most areas, winters are noticeably darker and have shorter days than the summer; wintertime is the time for added heat, and often the indoor air becomes markedly drier. Plants themselves differ in their growth rates: some grow throughout the year, and new shoots and leaves are always developing; others have a resting period in winter, brought on by the shortening darker days of fall. But, although these plants may use less water for growth while they are resting, the drier winter atmosphere may actually increase water loss from their leaves, and so increase their demand for it.

AIR-CONDITIONING AND WATERING

The drier air that prevails once the air-conditioning is turned on for the hot summer months will affect indoor plants' need for water. With longer summer days and stronger daylight, growth is likely to be more rapid. Both faster growth and drier air indicate a need for more frequent watering. Check soil moisture content, and let the plants guide watering at all times.

PLANTS IN FLOWER

The moisture balance of plants in full flower is usually more critical than that of foliage plants. Many flowers are more tender than their leaves, and petals lose water very rapidly; they are the first tissues to suffer from a water deficit. If left to dry even once, the calceolaria or cineraria will suffer irreversible damage, even though part of the plant recovers after the soil is remoistened. Most flowering plants, therefore, need to have their soil kept uniformly moist though not wet while they are in flower. Variations on how frequently to water after flowering are noted in the individual sections (pages 22 through 126).

FERTILIZER

Plants brought into the home or office from the greenhouse are moving to an environment where light is less intense, so growth will be slower. Most plants already have sufficient fertilizer in their soil to sustain top growth indoors for up to three months, longer during fall and winter. In low or moderate light situations, the slower-growing indoor plants may never need added fertilizer; the fresh soil mix that's used every few years during repotting (page 10) provides whatever is needed to maintain new growth. But in brighter situations as well as for flowering and seasonal plants, and culinary herbs whose leaves and shoots are used in food preparation, added fertilizer will help support attractive and useful development.

Even though new plants continue to grow vigorously, it is wise to wait at least a month before fertilizing. Let the plant adjust to its new environment. Newly potted plants need a similar adjustment time so new roots can replace those that were damaged during repotting.

Once plants have settled in their new environment, vigorous new growth will indicate that fertilization can begin. Guidelines for fertilizing each plant are given with the care information on pages 22 through 126.

It is easier to feed a number of plants at the same time, and schedules can be combined. Apply fertilizer to most indoor plants every 1-2 months while growth is rapid, and once or twice only during slower or no-growth times — usually the winter months. Alternatively, apply less plant food more often, to accommodate plants like ferns and African violets (*Saintpaulia*) that can be injured by full strength fertilizer; for these and many others, the recommendation is to fertilize at half the recommended strength. Some especially tender plants are best with the even more dilute, quarter strength fertilizer.

Fertilize annuals, seedlings, and young actively growing plants more frequently: about every three weeks during times of maximum growth (March through October), and every month to six weeks in winter. Some flowering plants like the azalea and those which are enjoyed for a season of only a few weeks will not require any additional fertilizer while they are in flower. Still others, whose growth continues even while they bear blossoms, continue to respond to regular fertilizing.

Type of fertilizer

Plant roots take up nutrients as chemical compounds which are the same for each nutrient regardless of source — organic or inorganic. For general indoor plant use, either can be used.

Fertilizers are available as liquid, powder, solids (tablet or spike form), and as granules or pellets. Soluble compounds are easy to apply and show quicker results than solids or slow release pellets. Simply add the fertilizer solution in place of water at normal watering time.

The soil should be slightly damp when fertilizer, either solid or liquid, is added. This avoids chemical burning of dry roots and the chance of missing the roots entirely if the fertilizer solution runs through cracks. Water bone-dry plants before adding fertilizer.

Use **liquid** fertilizers at or weaker than the recommended strength of dilution — never stronger. All newly rooted cuttings, seedlings, and young plants, as well as many indoor plant varieties, benefit from weaker solutions to avoid burning sensitive young roots.

Apply **dry** fertilizers at or less than the recommended level. The compounds must dissolve in soil moisture before roots can absorb them, so soil should be adequately moist. Follow the package directions.

For most indoor plants an N-P-K analysis ratio close to 1-1-1 or 1-2-1 will maintain balanced growth. Available percentages of the three major plant nutrients (nitrogen (N), phosphorus (P) in the form of phosphoric acid, and potassium (K)) are displayed on the fertilizer label. The ratio of these major nutrients affects the type and quality of plant growth. African Violets do best with a mix containing more nitrogen (higher first number). Special preparations of fertilizers are available for the acid-loving plants like azalea and gardenia. For annuals, herbs and other garden plants growing in hanging containers, use an outdoor fertilizer with a higher proportion of nitrogen.

Various components are included in a good soil mix. These can include (from left to right) perlite, vermiculite (see page 12), sand, and peat moss.

REPOTTING HOUSE PLANTS

Small, immature plants grow rapidly, and regular repotting is necessary to give roots more space for their development. Seedlings and young rooted cuttings may need repotting as often as every month. Full-grown plants develop more slowly. Vigorous indoor plants need repotting every year or two, in early spring just before a new flush of growth starts. Mature plants are repotted when necessary; this may be as often as every three, or as rarely as every ten years.

With good watering practices and fertilization as needed, long-term house plants need relatively little soil to support their top growth. Repotting is necessary when a plant becomes potbound, or if it has been overpotted, or to replace poor soil.

• A **potbound or rootbound** plant needs frequent watering, even though the root ball is soaked thoroughly every time; its new growth decreases in size; and its lower leaves turn prematurely yellow, even though they receive sufficient light.

To check the roots, invert the container and gently ease the plant out, without pulling; support the root ball with one hand. If necessary, tap the container rim on the edge of a table or countertop; a blunt knife, slid around the inside edge of the pot, will help release a sticking root ball. Most indoor plants will have roots at the edge of the soil ball, but a solid mass of fibrous or fleshy roots is an indication that repotting is needed.

Before repotting, water the plant in its present container so the rootball is moistened. It will be easier to moisten the whole new root ball if water can penetrate both fresh and original soil without difficulty.

Replant in the next size container, increasing width and depth by 1-2" (2.5-5cm).

• An **overpotted** plant is one in too large a container. The plant shows signs of root damage through leaves that wilt or die even while the soil seems to be moist, and loss of foliage and flowers. Carefully separate the original rootball from the abundance of repotting soil in the over-large container. The rootball may be bone dry if the new soil did not make good contact or if it was dry when previously repotted; or it may be perpetually wet. Moisten it, or let it start to dry out, and then replant in a pot that is just slightly larger than the rootball.

• **Poor soil** is usually slow to drain and so finely textured that air cannot get in. As soil particles become finer, the level of soil drops in the container. The more closely packed soil has reduced air spaces and healthy roots eventually die. Gently wash as much of the poor soil from the roots, and repot with fresh soil in a clean container.

Planting

In all containers with drainage holes, arch one or more pieces of broken clean pot over the holes so soil does not wash out or clog them. For containers without drainage holes, a layer of coarse material such as small stones, unmilled sphagnum moss, or charcoal under the soil acts as a buffer against overwatering.

Over the broken pot and/or buffer layer, add some new potting mixture without tamping it down, so that the top of the plant's new root ball will end up one-half to one inch (1.0 to 2.5cm) below the rim of the new pot. Containers larger than 10" (25cm) in diameter can have more space at the top. The final soil surface, or top of the new root ball, should be no higher on the plant than before. Most indoor plants have no roots at the top of their soil; some of the spent soil should be replaced with fresh and the root ball can be lifted slightly in its new pot to encourage lower root development.

Remove the plant from its old pot by inverting and tapping the rim if necessary. Large plants can be more easily removed from their containers by tipping it on its side and gripping the stems or trunk close to the soil line.

If roots are matted, gently loosen them — especially at the bottom. This frees up the growing root tips and allows quick new growth into the fresh soil.

Set the root ball on fresh soil in the new pot, and add fresh soil between and around bare roots. Center the plant and hold it in position while adding soil to the top of the root ball. A very large plant may require two hands for support, and repotting can be a two-person task.

Tamp down the soil with a stick or your fingertips, but don't compress it. Add more fresh soil to the same level as the original soil surface, and firm the whole potfull downwards to leave a watering space of one-half to one inch (1.0 to 2.5cm) (more for larger containers). A sharp rap of the filled pot on the table or ground helps settle fresh soil around the root ball without compressing it.

Water thoroughly several times to be sure no air pockets remain, and that all the soil (both fresh and original) is moistened together. This is critical, since roots cannot grow into fresh soil if it does not make intimate contact with the original. Check that water is draining out at the bottom and discard it.

Treat all newly potted and repotted plants with care, placing as little stress on them as possible. Their roots need time to recover and to grow new root hairs for water and nutrient uptake; many of the fragile root hairs are lost when the roots are handled during potting. For the first week or two, reduce water loss by keeping the plants in shadier and slightly cooler conditions. Do not fertilize for the first two to four weeks, even if new growth is made.

Grip the stems and trunks of large plants close to the soil line.

Growing Medium

House plants require soil that is porous and well-drained yet retains sufficient moisture that frequent watering is not needed. Various components are included in a good soil mix to achieve this balance. Perlite improves aeration and keeps the soil from becoming packed down. Rinse perlite before using to remove fluorides that will damage sensitive plants. Sand (sharp or coarse grade, not seashore) also improves aeration while adding to physical weight — useful to help anchor tall plants, but not a benefit in hanging containers. Peat moss is a major constituent of many mixes: a good horticultural grade is brown and chunky and will not be compacted by water. Dry, solid-packed peat moss should be crumbled and moistened before mixing with other soil components. Substitute shredded pine bark for peat moss when possible; other replacements (sawdust, compost) decompose more rapidly, and soil will need to be replaced more often.

The same **general indoor mix** can be used for most house plants: it consists of two parts peat moss or substitute, and one part sharp sand. For a general indoor mix containing soil, combine equal parts (by volume) of sterilized soil, peat moss or shredded pine bark, and sharp sand. Replace the sand with rinsed perlite for a lightweight mix, with or without soil.

The general indoor mix is then varied to come closer to the content and texture of the soil in which plants are already growing, and to meet the needs of new plants. Add an equal volume of peat moss or shredded pine bark for the **humusy indoor mix** that is useful for some ferns (page 15); increase the sand portion for a **sandy indoor mix** for plants that need a drier mix, like certain bromeliads and most cacti (pages 14, 15). Acid-loving plants like gardenia and hydrangea grow best in **acid to neutral indoor mix**, with pH lower than 7.0 (neutral): add aluminum sulfate if needed to reduce alkalinity.

Packaged soil mixes are often fine for an individual plant's need for fine or coarse texture. For larger containers use or add coarser humus components like fir bark or chopped osmunda fiber, gravel or chunks of unglazed clay pot or brick.

CONTAINERS

Plant containers are as varied as the plants they hold: clay, ceramic, glass, plastic or wood pots or bowls, for single specimens or for whole groups of plants together. Wicker baskets can also be used if a liner is placed inside to prevent soil and water from leaking out. The container markedly affects how often a plant will need water; for example, the water loss through the sides of a clay pot is about three times that from a plastic pot where most of the loss is from the soil surface. It's easier to overwater plants in plastic than in porous clay pots, and soil mixes for plastic containers should be light and open-structured to permit adequate aeration and drainage.

Soak new clay pots in plain water overnight or for at least several hours before use. Used pots of all kinds should be washed well to avoid any carry-over of disease organisms and chemical (salts) accumulations. Sterilize washed pots with boiling water, and let them stand in a solution containing half a cup of chlorine bleach per gallon of water (^{1}/2C per gal, 250ml per 4 liters); rinse before using.

VACATIONS

With a few preparations, indoor plants can be left untended for several days and even weeks at a time. Aim to reduce light, temperature, and water loss. Move plants away from direct sun and strong light. Turn down the thermostat in winter, or move to a cooler, shaded, or north-facing room in summer. Reduce water loss from plants by increasing the relative humidity around them: group them together. Wrap a plastic bag around each pot to prevent water loss from the soil and through the container; very small plants and cuttings can be placed inside a large plastic bag with supports to hold the plastic away from the leaves. Leave one end open to prevent excessive condensation.

CLEANING AND TRIMMING

Long-term house plants tend to get dusty, and dusty leaves are not attractive. Wash plants with glossy or simply smooth leaves, like philodendron and English ivy (*Hedera*) with plain water whenever necessary. The shower, bathtub, sink, patio or lawn (as weather permits) are useful for rinsing with water as well as for washing off unwanted pests and for leaching. Larger plants can be wiped with a moist soft cloth. Furry-leaved plants like purple passion vine (*Saxifraga sarmentosa*) and African violet (*Saintpaulia*) are best cleaned with a soft dry brush.

Just as outdoor plants need periodic pruning and thinning, so indoor plants benefit from trimming. Most obvious is the removal of unattractive dead leaves which are easy targets for airborne diseases. Some plants, like poinsettias (*Euphorbia pulcherrima*) and figs (*Ficus*), shed their dead leaves; others including cane-type plants like aglaonema, dracaena, dieffenbachia, and the palms retain dead foliage. Cut off the withered leaves with a sharp knife or scissors.

Shaping indoor plants varies from trimming the vigorous vines of plants like German ivy (*Senecio macroglossus*), wandering Jew (*Zebrina*), and grape ivy (*Cissus rhombifolia*), to pruning woody plants like azalea (*Rhododendron*) and weeping fig (*Ficus benjamina*). All involve the removal of living shoots. Some plants, notably figs and poinsettias, exude white latex sap that can be messy if it drops where it isn't wanted. The weeping wounds heal quickly; woody cuts are best left to form their own calluses to avoid sealing in pathogens with wound 'protection' compounds.

Since hanging plants are usually suspended at or above eye level, with all-round exposure, regular maintenance is important. Trailing plants like pothos (*Epipremnum aureum*), as well as spreading bushy ones like maidenhair ferns (*Adiantum*), need periodic trimming to maintain the desired size and form. This will encourage vigorous new growth as well as reduce the overlapping foliage that tends to crowd out other parts of the plant.

PLANTS OUTDOORS IN SUMMER

A porch, semi-shaded border, or other partly sheltered position provide excellent locations for indoor plants in warmer weather. Move plants out when the night temperatures stay above 50°F (10°C). This is the time for grooming, washing, leaching, and repotting if necessary. Plants that are to remain indoors through the summer can also be 'spring-cleaned' out of doors, in a semi-shaded, protected location.

Of those staying outdoors, tall plants and vines will need extra support as well as shelter from wind. Heavy rains can damage delicate leaves; plan for overhead protection as needed.

Move plants back indoors before nights get as cool as 45° (7°C) again. Before taking them inside, it is a good plan to wash them again to remove most insects and disease spores which, in the rarefied indoor climate, could multiply and grow alarmingly.

Plants can be propagated by a number of methods.

PROPAGATION — RENEWING HOUSE PLANTS

Most house plants offer material for more plants. With some, the method is obvious: spider plants *(Chlorophytum)* produce baby spiders; and wandering Jew *(Zebrina)* has long leafy stems that root easily in water or moist soil. Others can be propagated with relative ease from leaves *(Begonia rex)*, stem cuttings (jade plant, *Crassula*), and stem sections (dumb came, *Dieffenbachia)*. Propagation helps rejuvenate aging or overgrown plants.

Late winter, spring, and early summer are ideal times to start new house plants. The lengthening days and stronger natural light at this time stimulate a burst of new growth in all plants, both indoors and out. However, healthy cuttings can and should be started more or less successfully at any time if, for example, roots have been damaged through overwatering or high salts, and top growth is faltering.

The propagation medium is usually a general indoor plant mix that is capable of holding moisture close to the potential new plants while allowing air to penetrate to developing roots. Equal volumes of peat moss and vermiculite work well. Other rooting media include such components as sphagnum moss, sand, vermiculite alone, and perlite. Most light, soft, or fleshy stems will root quickly in any moist medium or in water. Heavier stems of geranium *(Pelargonium)*, and woody stems like those of the India rubber plant *(Ficus decora)* and croton *(Codiaeum)* will root more quickly if a rooting hormone is applied to the cut and callused surfaces.

Most cuttings root well at normal indoor temperatures. Electric heating cables encourage root development from woody cuttings and others that are slow to root; optimum soil temperature for rooting is about 70°F (21°C).

Increased humidity around cuttings and other unrooted plant parts helps reduce water loss and keeps stems and leaves turgid. But too much moisture can weaken soft tissues and permit the invasion of fungus infections. Provide adequate humidity, but allow some ventilation too.

Once rooted, young plants should be transferred to their proper mix so they will develop normally.

A **stem cutting** may or may not include the tip bud: even though an axillary bud (in the leaf axil, where leaf stem joins main stem) is not visible, so long as at least one leaf or leaf scar is included, roots will develop. Trim off lower leaves so that about one-third of the stem is bare. Slender, soft-stemmed cuttings such as pothos *(Epipremnum aureum)* or wandering Jew *(Zebrina)* can be pushed into moist growing medium as soon as they are cut from the parent plant. Heavier and woody stems like those of geranium *(Pelargonium)*, hydrangea, and croton *(Codiaeum)* are best left to dry in air for an hour or more; dust cut ends with rooting powder before pushing into moist soil.

Stem sections greatly increase the yield of new plants from thick, woody plants. The stem cutting is cut into sections, each section including at least one leaf whose axillary bud will grow into the new shoot. Place sections right side up, with the upper cut end out of the rooting medium. Apply rooting hormone only to the lower, buried end.

Leaf cuttings are used to propagate plants that grow in rosettes or whose stems are too short for stem cuttings.
• Some leaf cuttings include the leaf stem or petiole, and new plants develop close to the leaf blade of, say, a rosette peperomia or African violet *(Saintpaulia)*. For faster rooting, dust the stem with rooting hormone. Push the stem all the way into the rooting medium.
• A single leaf can be the source of several new plants when the blade itself, removed from the parent plant, is pinned onto the surface of moist rooting medium. Slit across some of the veins on the underside, and use bent wire, hairpins, or toothpicks to fasten the leaf blade flat, right side up on the medium. Leaf blade cuttings can be taken from fancy-leaved begonia and many gesneriads (page 16).
• Many succulents have fleshy, stemless leaves that will root when detached and placed in moist rooting medium. Push each leaf in to about one-third of its length, right side up. Some of these are the jade plant *(Crassula)*, kalanchoe, and sedum varieties.
• The fleshy leaves of snake plant *(Sansevieria)* can be cut into 2-4 inch (5-10cm) sections. Mark the top of each section so they can be planted right side up, and leave to dry in air before pressing into the rooting medium.

Air layering, the technique used to reduce the height of woody indoor plants like *Ficus* species, involves the removal of a thin layer of bark from the area of wood that is to be rooted — without cutting off the stem. The stem can be girdled with one or two cuts, removing about a quarter of an inch (0.6cm) of the bark. If the heavy stem has no bark, as on plants like dracaena and dumb cane *(Dieffenbachia)*, simply slice into about one-third of the stem and insert a tiny wedge to stop the edges from closing up. Apply rooting powder to the wounds of both woody and non-woody plants, and wrap round with damp whole sphagnum moss. Cover with plastic and secure each end with covered wire or plastic ties. The sphagnum must be kept moist at all times. Roots should become visible in several weeks (non-woody stems) or months (woody stems). At that time, cut right through the stem below the rooted portion and plant.

Divisions come from plants that form clumps, like many ferns as well as snake plants *(Sansevieria)* and African violets *(Saintpaulia)*. The bromeliads (page 14) often form offshoots, especially after flowering. Plantlets on stems or runners that grow from plants such as spider plants *(Chlorophytum)*, flame violets *(Episcia)*, and strawberry begonia *(Saxifraga sarmentosa)*, and at the leaf bases of the piggyback plant *(Tolmeiea menziesii)*. These can be rooted by pinning them to moist rooting medium before cutting from the parent plant, or they may be removed first and handled like tender stem cuttings. Separated bromeliad offshoots (pups) can be left to harden for several days, or they can be potted right away. Dust cut surfaces with rooting and fungicidal powder before planting. Keep newly planted offshoots lightly moist for several weeks while they form new roots.

Rhizomes and **tubers** provide sections for new plant development. Sometimes the rhizomes spread across the soil surface, and the parent plant doesn't have to be repotted in order to propagate. Let cut portions dry in air and then press into moist rooting medium. Plants that can be propagated from rhizomes and tubers include rex begonia and caladiums.

Allium schoenoprasum

THE CULINARY HERBS

Herbs add fragrance and flavor wherever they are grown, and a good range of them can be cultivated indoors. Although some mature plants tend to be more useful than decorative, young culinary herbs will remain relatively small and compact when planted in containers and the fresh leaves and shoots are harvested regularly. They provide useful alternatives or supplements to outdoor-grown herbs, filling in when the weather cuts back on garden production.

Grow herbs in windowsill boxes, shallow planters, pots and other containers, and/or hanging planters. Most can be started from seed. Use a general indoor mix that is slightly acid to neutral. Some prefer neutral to slightly alkaline soil: add limestone to reduce soil acidity. Good drainage is essential. Most prefer diffused bright light and cool to average temperatures. A kitchen windowsill often provides the needed relative humidity and is also handy for food preparation. Clean as needed by spraying with water.

The following herbs described in this book are especially suitable for growing in containers indoors:

Allium schoenoprasum Chives
Anethum graveolens Dill
Artemisia dracunculus Tarragon
Foeniculum vulgare Fennel
Melissa officinalis Lemon balm
Mentha Mint
Ocimum basilicum Basil
Origanum majorana Marjoram
Origanum vulgare Oregano
Petroselinum crispum Parsley
Poterium sanguisorba Salad burnet
Rosmarinus officinalis Rosemary
Salvia officinalis Sage
Satureja hortensis Savory, Summer
Satureja montana Savory, Winter
Thymus vulgaris, T. citriodorus Thyme

BROMELIADS

Bromeliads are easily grown, adaptable plants with exotic good looks. A broad spectrum of forms and sizes offers curved and pendulous stems, straight tubular vases, low starry clusters, and miniatures. Bromeliads can be grown in terrariums, regular pots, or in the air (epiphytic) like *Tillandsia*, the genus that includes Spanish moss. Their foliage is often bold and colorful, and many have brilliant, long-lasting flowers.

All bromeliads thrive with fresh air and warm indoor temperatures. Good air movement ensures that there are adequate supplies of carbon dioxide, nitrogen, and moisture for the air plants *(Tillandsia)* that often grow without soil or added water. Tank-type bromeliads like living vase *(Aechmea)*, that hold water in their central cups, are less dependent on circulating air. Water thoroughly, then let soil become partly dry before watering again. Excessive moisture can result in basal rot. Fill the cups of tank-type plants, letting them overflow so all the leaf bases receive water. Bromeliads growing without soil or other medium are watered by misting. Fertilize bromeliads regularly while they are growing, and less often if growth slows during winter months.

Most bromeliads grow best in water-retaining but not soggy growing media that are porous and neutral or slightly acid. Set each plant's crown at but not below the surface. Use a porous, slightly acid bromeliad mix containing equal volumes of sphagnum peat moss and perlite. Use broken pot (crocks) at the bottom of the container to assist drainage. Variations to this basic mix include added portions of chopped tree fern, redwood bark chips, shredded redwood bark, cypress mulch, leaf mold, topsoil, or sand.

The coarse bromeliad mix for dyckia and others whose soil should dry completely between waterings consists of two parts sharp sand with one part coarse gravel or crushed granite, and one part peat moss or leaf mold. This very coarse mix retains sufficient moisture while maintaining excellent drainage. The sandy indoor mix used for cacti is also fine for these bromeliads.

Species of the following bromeliads are especially suitable for growing indoors:

Aechmea Living-vase, Urn plant
Ananas Pineapple
Billbergia Friendship plant
Cryptanthus Earth star
Dyckia Dyckia
Guzmania Orange star, Scarlet star
Neoregelia Blushing bromeliad
Nidularium Birdnest plant
Tillandsia Air plant
Vriesea Flaming sword

Neoregelia carolinae

CACTI AND SUCCULENTS

Cacti and other succulent plants have very highly developed methods of water storage for survival in some of the most inhospitable conditions on earth. Many are native to hot, arid zones; they are often slow growing and adaptable. They include some of the most tolerant of house plants.

In keeping with their natural environments, the majority of cacti and succulents prefer bright light and warmth, while tolerating extremes of both. They grow best with seasonal changes like those experienced in desert areas: lower temperatures for the dry dormant season, and abundant though infrequent water supplies during the growing season. To simulate these conditions, water most cacti and succulents **thoroughly** when soil is dry. Soils for cacti vary from sandy or even gritty to humusy mixes for epiphytic plants. All need to be well-draining, and modifications of the general indoor mix (page 11) work well. For a sandy mix, add up to an equal volume of washed sharp sand. For a humusy mix, add the same volume of peat moss or other humus. Add fertilizer during the growing season. Specific details are given for each plant or plant group.

Cacti include some of the most tolerant of house plants.

FERNS

Ferns have long been popular for indoor decoration. Their gentle green foliage is an ideal contrast or complement to interior decor. The combination of ferns with other living plants is visually appealing and has the benefit of the naturally enhanced humidity that surrounds plant groups. Various ferns, from the bold staghorns *(Platycerium)* to the billowing Boston ferns *(Nephrolepis exaltata)*, can be grown in a wide range of indoor conditions with moderate to high relative humidity (40-50% and more). Some are able to grow well in drier locations with humidity under 40%. These are among the easiest of ferns, tolerating low light, winter sun, and occasionally dry soil as well as drier air. They include bird's-nest fern *(Asplenium nidus)*, holly ferns *(Cyrtomium falcatum* and cultivars), button fern *(Pellaea rotundifolia)*, some staghorns *(Platycerium)*, polypody ferns *(Polypodium)*, table ferns *(Pteris)*, and leatherleaf *(Rumohra adiantiformis)*.

Most ferns grow well in moderate light with filtered rather than direct sun. In more shaded positions, growth is slower and the older fronds turn yellow and dry out. Ferns adapt well to prevailing indoor temperatures, tolerating normal variations. Like other indoor plants, ferns will be damaged by hot and cold drafts and by sudden extreme changes in temperature. Water most ferns when the soil surface begins to dry.

Ferns can be grown in a wide range of indoor conditions.

A porous, humusy soil mix prevents overwatering. Add equal parts by volume of peat moss (or leaf mold) and sharp sand to one part of the general indoor mix (page 11) for a **basic fern mix**. Some ferns grow better in a **humus-rich fern mix** consisting of one part general indoor plant soil, two parts peat moss, one part leaf mold, and one part sharp sand or perlite. The leaf mold may be replaced with a 50-50 mixture of redwood bark chips and oak leaf mold. Good drainage helps avoid mold development. Fertilize actively growing ferns every 4-6 weeks, at one-quarter the recommended rate; do not fertilize when little or no new growth is seen. As an alternative, actively growing ferns can be fertilized with an even more dilute solution (such as one-tenth the recommended strength) at every watering. Regular leaching, at least once each year, is important.

Delicate fern fronds are particularly sensitive to chemicals and should not be misted with tapwater containing chlorine. However, rather than apply pesticides that would kill fronds outright, use a spray of water to remove mealybugs, aphids, or spider mites; scale insects may need to be removed by hand. Some damage will result, but new fronds soon grow. Ferns with thick, rapidly developing fronds like the Boston ferns *(Nephrolepis)* can be sheared back to soil level to renew the display.

All of the ferns in this book can be grown indoors, and copy for each (pages 22-126) highlights individual needs.

Adiantum Maidenhair fern
Asplenium Bird's-nest fern
Cyrtomium Holly fern
Davallia Hare's-foot fern
Nephrolepis Boston fern
Pellaea Button fern
Platycerium Staghorn fern
Polypodium Polypody fern
Polystichum Shield fern
Pteris Table fern
Rumohra Leather fern

Gesneriads' decorative value frequently lasts all year.

PALMS and CYCADS

A number of palms and palm-like cycads are adaptable and durable as house plants. Potted palms for table, pedestal, and floor specimens are young (sometimes juvenile) forms of tree palms used as accents or in groups for interiorscapes and malls. The versatility of palms is a valuable factor, both indoors and out. Even though most of them originate in tropical and subtropical areas, some are also quite hardy; they tolerate drier air and lower temperatures — even below freezing — when established in outdoor settings.

All palms tolerate shade, and young indoor palms often prefer it. For a general recommendation, moderate light levels are best. As palms mature, stronger light (not full sun) may be needed. Average to warm indoor temperatures are ideal for most, though a few are best in cooler areas. All palms need plenty of water when they are growing actively, usually from spring to fall. Keep the soil moist and fertilize once a month until growth slows in late fall. Good drainage, porous soil, and deep containers ensure that the palms' fleshy roots stay away from excess water which can drown them. During winter when growth stops or slows, fertilizer is not needed, and most palms should be allowed to become partly dry between waterings.

Soil for palms needs to be a well-draining, rich, humusy combination of equal parts of general indoor mix (page 11) and humus like peat moss, chopped tree fern, or chopped or shredded pine bark. For larger containers, use a coarser textured mix. To add weight that will anchor taller or wider palms, use crushed rock beneath the rootball.

These palm and palm-like plants are suited to indoor conditions. For further details, see individual plant descriptions.

Arecastrum Arecastrum
Caryota Fishtail palm
Chamaedorea Parlor palm
Chrysalidocarpus Bamboo palm
Cycas Sago palm
Howea Sentry palm
Livistona Chinese fan palm
Phoenix Date palm
Rhapis Lady palm
Zamia Cardboard palm

Rhapis excelsa

GESNERIADS

Gesneriads range in size from the smallest miniature African violets to the flowing, majestic *Aeschynanthus* vines. Their decorative value frequently lasts all year.

Most gesneriads need at least two to three hours of sun or bright light every day, and some require more than this for flowering. Average to warm temperatures are best, though many gesneriads also tolerate cooler nights. For most, let the soil become partly dry between waterings. African violets *(Saintpaulia)* and the more woody gesneriads like *Columnea* also survive an occasional drying out. Remoisten their dry soil with care, to ensure that the whole root ball is wet. Gesneriad soil needs to be open, porous, well draining, and, at the same time, finely textured. This requires a balanced texture that is fine enough for the development of delicate roots while still permitting air to be drawn in freely as excess water drains out. Poor drainage will result in root loss. A good **basic gesneriad mix**, with pH 6.0-7.0, consists of equal parts (by volume) of crumbled peat moss, perlite or sharp sand, and vermiculite. To reduce the acidity, add lime or ground eggshells at the rate of two level tablespoons per quart. A more humusy gesneriad mix contains one extra part of peat moss.

Of the more than sixty gesneriad genera that can be grown in containers, the following are most suitable for indoor culture.

Aeschynanthus Basket plant
Columnea Goldfish plant
Episcia Episcia
Nematanthus Pouch flower
Saintpaulia African violet
Sinningia Gloxinia
Streptocarpus Cape primrose

PESTS, DISORDERS, and DISEASES

Pests of Plants Indoors

The most common house plant pests are spider mites, mealybugs, scale insects, whitefly, and aphids. In addition, thrips and leaf miners may damage some indoor flowering plants. Soil pests, like springtails and fungus gnats occur on all container-grown plants where the soil or container has not been thoroughly sterilized.

The outdoor use of house plants periodically exposes them to all garden pests such as caterpillars, slugs, snails, and thrips. These may thrive once the plants are moved back indoors. For this reason, plants which are being moved in from outdoors should first be washed thoroughly with a spray of clear water. A thorough watering is also recommended to leach out excess soluble salts and to make sure the soil is uniformly moist before bringing plants indoors. Check, too, for larger pests that may have settled underneath the pots.

Despite the best control programs employed by growers and retailers, it sometimes happens that a new plant harbors pests whose eggs have survived. A period of isolation for 10-14 days is sufficient for most common pests to hatch and develop. Adult pests are often easier to see than are their eggs. Most problems can be eliminated before the plant is combined with others.

A few pests may not show up in this short a time, being present in minute numbers until the indoor climate becomes more favorable for their development. Spider mites, for example, can be carried undetected into the house on plants. A small number will survive while conditions are moist and humid. When the environment becomes drier the mites multiply alarmingly, causing major damage and defying all attempts to wash them off.

Regular checks for abnormal growth and the presence of insects can be combined with checks for watering needs. Most pests lurk under leaves and close to the growing tips where tissue is softest. Most of them can be washed off with a spray of water or an insecticidal soap applied in either in a well-ventilated area like the garage, or outdoors. Several washes over a period of two or three weeks, plus isolation for the infested plant, generally solves the problem. Chemical sprays are not pleasant to use, and are often recommended for outdoor application only -- if at all. Aerosols are hazardous, not only to the general environment but to plant tissues which can be burned by the propellant if the nozzle is held closer than 24" (60cm). Ferns are particularly sensitive to all chemicals and badly infested fronds are best removed and destroyed.

A number of natural, organic pest controls are now available. Pyrethrum (Pyrethrin), derived from a chrysanthemum or tanacetum, is one of the safest compounds. Its synthetic form is Resmethrin. Both are reasonably effective against many common insect pests, and are less likely than other chemicals to damage tender blossoms of flowering plants. If possible, avoid spraying any chemicals on flowers. Other compounds recommended for indoor plants are safe when used with care on green plants, or on flowering plants before the flowers open.

House Plant Disorders

Many house plants tolerate a range of conditions, but sooner or later all will display the effects of some factor that damages or infects. A plant disorder usually results from cultural stress, and sometimes the possible causes are two extremes of the same factor; for example, watering too much and too little both lead to wilting leaves.

If one or more plants show symptoms of disorder, first check the soil. This is the best guide to the most frequent plant troubles for established plants. Recently moved plants may have problems that result from too much or too little light. Other plant disorders are caused by very dry air (usually in winter), hot or cold drafts, insufficient fertilizer, and potbound roots. In some cases, diseases cause symptoms similar to those caused by cultural stress.

Diseases that affect house plants

Although relatively rare among house plants that stand apart from other plants, infections can quickly develop in the warmth and high humidity that frequently prevail where several or many plants are grouped together. Plants are most vulnerable to airborne and soil-borne disease organisms when they are stressed. High soluble salts, a move to a new location, or the presence of dead plant tissues on healthy ones all create stresses for the plant.

Bacterial and fungal rots and spots are the usual infections. Virus diseases and nematode (eelworm) infestations have generally been eliminated long before plants are marketed, and are almost never seen outside the major production areas for indoor plants.

Bacterial rots may be systemic, with the ability to affect almost any weak part of the infected plant. Or they may be localized, in which case reinfection can be avoided if infected parts are removed promptly. All bacteria thrive in warm, moist to damp, close conditions. Unhealthy soft or weak plant tissues are most vulnerable. Once active, bacteria are spread through contaminated hands and tools, in soil, and on warm moist air currents.

Symptoms of bacterial infection are pale green, yellow, or water-soaked leaf areas that become dry patches of dark brown or black with yellowish margins. In more severe cases, plant stems are affected.

Systemic bacteria develop from inside and are carried right through a plant in its water-conducting tissues. Infected plants must be completely burned or otherwise destroyed to remove all of the systemic bacteria. The container and tools should be sterilized, and hands washed with soap before healthy plants are touched.

Localized bacterial infections are easier to control. Remove badly affected parts and alter the growing conditions. If a plant has recently been moved to an area of lower light where it cannot grow so fast, it has less need for water and fertilizer; any excesses encourage the development of leaf spot diseases. The best protection is good aeration, lower temperatures, and a reduced fertilization schedule (or none) until balanced plant health is re-established.

Fungal rots include powdery mildew, the water mold rots that are soil- and water-borne, root and stem rots, and leaf spots and blights. As with bacteria, fungi can be avoided by keeping plants clean and healthy, with good aeration, and through prompt removal of fading tissues. They are similarly spread, through overwatering and splashing water. Stressed plants are most susceptible. Chemical controls are available, though improved conditions and removal of infected plant parts is usually enough for plants indoors. Provide more space for air circulation, or move infected plants to a drier place. Fungicidal soaps, dips, and other treatments are also available.

Virus infections are systemic and are spread through unsterilized soil or by sucking insects like aphids and leafhoppers. Symptoms are irregular lighter color or dark yellow areas on leaves, and plants may be stunted and/or deformed. Nematodes also cause deformed, stunted growth, as well as distinct knots or enlarged nodes on the roots. In either case, the affected plants are best discarded and the source (if known) avoided for future plant stock.

COMMON PESTS OF PLANTS INDOORS

Pest	Typical Damage	Control
SPIDER MITES	Tiny white or yellow spots on leaves, later becoming mottled and dusty. Fine webs under leaves and in growing tips. Leaves may curl up. Thrive in dry climates.	Wash and spray with clean warm water several times in 2-3 weeks. Apply insecticidal soap as recommended. Spray Kelthane, Dimite, or other miticide.*
SCALE INSECTS	Clustered or single green to brown scales under leaves and on stems, plus mottling of foliage when seen against the light.	Rub off scales with moist cotton swab or (for stout leaves like many bromeliads) soft toothbrush. Or wipe with cotton soaked in rubbing alcohol (check plant for tolerance by treating one leaf, then wait 24 hours). Apply insecticidal soap as recommended. Spray Malathion or Cygon 2E;* rinse with water after 24 hours; repeat one week later.
MEALYBUGS	Cottony white secretions along stems and under leaves. Small, flat insects move, though slowly.	Wash off insects and secretions with clean warm water. Kill by wiping with rubbing alcohol—first check plant's tolerance. Apply insecticidal soap as recommended. Spray with insecticide containing Pyrethrum, Malathion or Diazinon.*
APHIDS	Green, red or black insects visibly sucking plant juices. Cause small, distorted, weak growth.	Wash whole plant several times. Apply insecticidal soap as recommended. Spray with insecticide containing Pyrethrum or Malathion.*
WHITEFLY	Tiny white moth-like insects fly up when plant is disturbed. Larvae suck plant juices, causing general weakening. Thrive in dry climates, generally on flowering plants.	Wash off tiny wingless larvae. Apply insecticidal soap as recommended. Control adult whitefly with spray of insecticide containing Pyrethrum or Malathion.*
LEAF MINERS	Irregular yellow, cream or brown channels across leaves.	Spray with insecticide containing Malathion.*
THRIPS	Thin, papery scars on leaves remain after insects have sucked plant juices.	Apply insecticidal soap as recommended. Control thrips with insecticide containing Pyrethrum or Malathion.*
SPRINGTAILS	Transparent jumping insects at soil surface. Some damage to lower plant tissues.	Water with mild vinegar solution to discourage springtails (1-2 Tbsp per pint, or 11-21 ml or 3/4-1 1/2 Tbsp per liter). Or apply solution of Pyrethrum or Malathion to soil.*
FUNGUS GNATS	Tiny black insects fly up in clouds when disturbed. White maggots (larvae) come to moist soil surface.	Water with dilute (not spray strength) solution of Pyrethrum or Malathion.*

* Check with supplier for safest recommended compounds, and apply according to manufacturers' directions.

DISORDERS AND DISEASES OF PLANTS INDOORS

Symptom	Possible causes
BUDS FAIL TO OPEN, WITHER OR DROP OFF	• Insufficient light • Air too dry • Overwatering

PETAL & LEAF TIPS TURN BROWN	• Check soil:
	  if DRY, water more often or more thoroughly
	  if MOIST, cause may be high salts: LEACH soil (page 9)
	• Air too dry • Plant sensitive to fluorides (page 8)

LEAVES TURN YELLOW OR BROWN	• Check soil:
	  if DRY, water more often or more thoroughly
	  if MOIST, cause may be high salts: LEACH soil (page 9)
	  if WET, may be poor drainage or overwatering
	• Temperature too high • Air too dry • Insufficient fresh air
	• Plant sensitive to fluorides (page 8)

BROWN OR BLACK SPOTS ON PETALS & LEAVES	• Overwatering or poor drainage • Light too bright
	• Leaf spot disease (page 17):
	  FUNGI cause dry areas of bulls-eye spots or blotchy patches, some have black raised pustules.
	  BACTERIA cause soft water-soaked or oily areas that dry brown or black.

FLOWERS &/OR LEAVES ROLL OR CURL	• Hot or cold draft • Aphids
BUDS, FLOWERS &/OR LEAVES FALL	• Overwatering or poor drainage • Insufficient light • Soil very dry • Cold draft • Injury caused by household gas • Later stages of bacterial infection (page 17)
LEAVES PALE GREEN OR YELLOW	• Too little or too much light • Plant needs fertilizer • Temperature too high
NEW GROWTH THIN AND PALE	• Too little light • Too much nitrogen (N) in fertilizer/soil • Temperature too high
LEAVES PALE OR YELLOW WITH GREEN VEINS	• Plant needs fertilizer • Soil too alkaline (pH 9+), making iron unavailable: water using solution of 2 tsp lemon juice in 1 pint water (21 ml or 1$\frac{1}{2}$ Tsp per liter).
NEW LEAVES SMALL	• Plant needs repotting—check roots • Plant needs fertilizer • Injury caused by high salts: LEACH soil (page 9) • Temperature too high

PLANT WILTS	• Check soil:
	  if DRY, water more often or more thoroughly
	  if MOIST, cause may be high salts: LEACH soil (page 9)
	  if WET, may be poor drainage or overwatering
	• Plant needs repotting—check roots • Air too dry

WHOLE PLANT SUDDENLY COLLAPSES	• Roots dead, caused by water saturation and/or high salts (page 9) • Cold or hot draft • Bacterial infection
GROWTH STUNTED	• Roots dying, caused by water saturation and/or high salts (page 9)
DISTORTED LEAVES, ABNORMAL GROWTH	• Weedkiller injury • Virus infection (page 17)
ROOTS APPEAR ON SOIL SURFACE	• Roots may be waterlogged or completely dry in lower part of container • Plant needs repotting—check roots below surface
PLANT ROTS AT OR JUST ABOVE SOIL	• Too much water, caused by overwatering or poor drainage • Too cold

GUIDE TO HOUSE PLANTS: PLANT DESCRIPTIONS

The indoor plants described on the following pages are arranged alphabetically by botanical name. Common name or names are given with each entry, and both common and botanical names are indexed on pages 128 through 136.

At least one full color photograph illustrates every genus or group of plants. In groups with several to many cultivars or varieties, the best and most readily available are described.

These pages include a wide variety of house plants. Each is shown with one or more symbols for rapid identification of the plant or plant group's cultural needs.

SYMBOLS FOR A PLANTS CULTURAL NEEDS

LIGHT for indoor plants (page 6)

LL - LOW LIGHT: prefers or performs well in low light conditions, or shade.

ML - MODERATE LIGHT: prefers or performs well in partial shade or diffused light.

BL - BRIGHT LIGHT: prefers or performs well in full sun or bright indirect light.

HUMIDITY (page 7)

H - Best with relative humidity 50% or more.

TEMPERATURE (page 7)

CA - COOL to AVERAGE TEMPERATURES: days 60-75°F (16-24°C), nights as cool as 45°F (7°C).

WA - AVERAGE to WARM TEMPERATURES: days 70-80°F (21-27°C), nights 60-65°F (16-18°C).

WATERING (page 8)

MS - Keep soil moist.

PD - Let soil become partly dry between waterings.

DS - Allow soil to dry out between thorough waterings.

Acalypha hispida

Abutilon pictum 'Thompsonii'

Acalypha wilkesiana

ABUTILON (a-BEW-ti-lon) BL - CA - MS
Flowering Maple, Parlor Maple, Indian Mallow
Shrubby flowering plants with bell-shaped blossoms in orange, red, salmon, yellow, or white. Foliage dark green or variegated, often lobed and maple-like. Flowers from spring to fall, continuing all year with adequate light. Container plants for bright, airy indoor locations; useful summer color in partial shade outdoors. Grow in general indoor mix; repot if needed in early spring. Propagate in summer from stem cuttings; in spring sow seed of green-leaved varieties.
MAINTENANCE Avoid direct scorching sun. Trim back rapidly growing shoots to encourage bushiness. Prune larger plants in spring, reducing last year's growth for shape and strength. Fertilize at half recommended strength every 2-4 weeks in spring and summer; every 1-3 months in fall and winter when growth is less rapid. Leach regularly to avoid damaging accumulation of soluble salts. Check for spider mites, whitefly, mealybugs, and scale insects.

A. ×hybridum (HYB-ri-dum)
Chinese-lantern
Shapely flowering shrub grows to height and spread of 4' (1.2m) or more. Big, colorful flowers, dark green or variegated leaves. Many named cultivars.

A. megapotamicum (me-ga-po-TAM-i-kum)
Trailing Abutilon, Weeping Chinese-lantern
Pendulous, lantern-like flowers on graceful stems with slender foliage. Good basket plants.
'Variegata' (ve-ri-e-GAH-ta): green and yellow variegated leaves.

A. pictum 'Thompsonii' (PIK-tum)
[A. striatum 'Thompsonii' (stry-AH-tum)]
Spotted Flowering Maple
Handsome shrub can grow to 15' (4.5m). Broad, yellow mottled leaves and salmon-orange flowers.

ACALYPHA (a-KAL-i-fa) BL - WA - H - PD
Tender, fast-growing leafy or flowering shrubs for colorful indoor accents. Grow in humusy indoor mix; repot in spring at pruning time. Vigorous roots. Propagate in summer and fall from stem cuttings.
MAINTENANCE Avoid direct scorching sun. Trim rapidly growing shoots to encourage branching; prune several times during growth to maintain desired shape and size. To renew straggly plants, cut tops back to 12" (30cm) in spring. Fertilize at half recommended strength every 4-6 weeks while growth is rapid; every 3-4 months in fall and winter. Leaves curl when humidity is too low, drop when soil is too wet or too dry. Check for spider mites and whitefly.

Adiantum hispidulum

Adiantum raddianum 'Ocean Spray'

Adiantum raddianum 'Microphyllum'

Adiantum raddianum 'Pacific Maid'

A. hispida (HIS-pi-da)
Chenille Plant, Foxtail, Red-hot Cattail
Showy, pendulous tassel-like clusters of red or purple flowers from late spring to fall. Fast growing shrub for pots and tubs. Smaller form ideal for hanging baskets. After flowering, prune to encourage strong new branch development.

A. wilkesiana 'Macafeeana' (wilk-see-AH-na ma-ka-fee-AH-na)
Copperleaf, Jacob's-coat
Colorful red foliage with crimson and bronze markings. Rapid growth to height and spread of 2-5' (0.6-1.5m). Use as annual outdoors.

ADIANTUM (a-dee-AN-tum)   ML - CA - H - MS
Maidenhair Fern
Dainty, delicate ferns for moist atmospheres. Good in unbroken north light or filtered east light. Fast growing. Rhizomes and fibrous roots. Grow in pots or baskets with humusy indoor or basic fern mix; small plants in terrariums. Propagate by division when repotting in spring.
MAINTENANCE Water to keep soil lightly moist; do not let plants wilt. Mist with plain water to clean foliage; avoid chemicals. Fertilize at one-quarter recommended strength every 4-6 weeks, or with weaker solution at every watering while growth is active. Delicate roots can be damaged by stronger applications. As growth slows reduce watering, stop fertilizing, and set plant in cooler area. Cut off old and discolored fronds. Check for slugs and snails on plants moved in from shade outdoors, and for spider mites, mealybugs, and scale insects.

A. 'Birkenheadii': upright, five-fingered divided fronds are light green.

A. 'Ming Maidenhair': compact, tightly clustering fronds with cool green fan-shaped leaflets.

A. hispidulum (his-PID-ew-lum)
Australian Maidenhair, Pink Maidenhair, Rough Maidenhair
Grows about 12" (30cm) high. Spreading five-fingered fronds rosy bronze when young, maturing medium green.

A. raddianum (rah-dee-AH-num)
Delta Maidenhair
Triangular (deltoid) fronds with fan-like leaflets on black stems. Compact or spreading forms, height 10-18" (25-45cm).
'Fritz-Luthii': steel-blue leaflets, vigorous growth.
'Microphyllum' (my-kroh-FIL-um), **Baby's-tears:** airy, billowing fern, minute wedge-shaped leaflets rarely exceed 1/8" (3mm). Best with higher humidity than other maidenhairs.

Adiantum tenerum

Adiantum trapeziforme

Aechmea chantinii

A. raddianum cultivars (cont.):
'Ocean Spray': compact fern with overlapping fronds. Light, fluffy, look. New growth delicate light green.
'Pacific Maid': compact, upright growth. Leaflets yellow-green when young, mature satiny dark green.

A. tenerum cultivars (TEN-e-rum)
Brittle Maidenhair, Fan Maidenhair Fern
Triangular or oval fronds can grow to 36" (90cm) long.
'Farleyense' (far-lee-EN-see), **Barbados Maidenhair, Glory Fern:** showy arching and drooping fronds may be tinted rose.
'Scutum' (SKEW-tum) ['Wrightii' (RY-tee-y)]: graceful fronds are pink when young, mature fresh green. Height to 20" (50cm).

A. trapeziforme (tra-pee-zi-FOR-me)
Giant Maidenhair
Black stems separate 2" (5cm) long, brilliant green leaflets on 18" (45cm) fronds. Bold yet fragile appearance; robust fern for moist areas.

TO LEACH PLANTS — Water well four or five times in succession, discarding all drainage water. For a more thorough leaching, saturate the soil by immersing the whole container almost to its brim; leave to soak for 10-15 minutes; remove, and allow soil to drain. Repeat several times.

AECHMEA (EEK-mee-a)   **ML - WA - PD**
Living-vase, Urn Plant
Long-lasting bromeliads. Flowers and fruits rise in colorful clusters above stiff or succulent foliage. Best leaf color in diffused bright light. Easy to grow; tolerate shade. Small, fleshy root system; rarely need repotting. Grow in porous, slightly acid bromeliad mix with fir bark or chopped osmunda fibers. Propagate in late spring by offsets or seed. Many species and varieties offer wide range of form and size.
Reported effective in tests to freshen or purify air (page 4).
AFTER FLOWERING, young plants, or offsets, develop at plant base. When 2-4" (5-10cm) high, cut from mature parent plant and pot.
MAINTENANCE Keep water in central cup at all times; water softer-leaved, succulent living-vases more often than stiff-leaved specimens. Mist gray-coated foliage every few days to provide more water for growth. Clean with soft brush or gentle spray of warm water. Fertilize at one-quarter recommended strength, adding solution to soil and cup every 4 weeks. Provide relative humidity 30% or more; brown leaf tips indicate dry air. Trim damaged, discolored parts. Mulch with fir bark to support newly potted or top-heavy plants. Check for scale insects, mealybugs, and basal rot.

Aechmea fasciata

Aechmea fasciata 'Variegata'

Aechmea fosteriana

Aechmea luddemanniana 'Mend'

Aechmea orlandiana 'Ensign'

A. chantinii (shan-TIN-ee-y)
Amazonian Zebra Plant
Stiff, spiny, olive green leaves with cross-bands. Height 18-24" (45-60cm). Branched cluster of yellow-and-red blossoms in winter, lasts 4-6 weeks. Tolerates some full sun, adding reddish hue to foliage.

A. fasciata (fa-see-AH-ta)
Silver Vase, Urn Plant
Reliable, easiest living-vase. Broad, stiff, silvery leaves. Height to 24" (60cm). Blue flowers in tight pink cluster that lasts 4-6 months.
'Albomarginata' (al-bo-mar-ji-NAH-ta), **White Margined Vase:** large variety with white-margined foliage.
'Variegata' (ve-ri-e-GAH-ta), **Variegated Silver Vase:** wide leaves have creamy-white central stripes.
A. ×fascini 'Friederika' (fas-KIN-y)
Broad green, lightly banded leaves; long-lasting flower cluster with red bracts. Height 24-30" (60-75cm). No spines. Tolerates shade.

A. fosteriana (fos-te-ree-AH-na)
Narrow, tubular rosette rises to 24" (60cm) with 4-8" (10-20cm) spread. Purplish brown zig-zag bands on olive green leaves. Yellow and crimson flower cluster on long, arching stem. Best in very bright diffused light; good corner plant near window.

A. luddemanniana (loo-de-ma-nee-AH-na)
Large formal plant can spread to 36" (90cm). Dark green leaves turn bronze-purple in very bright light. Tall cluster of lavender flowers followed by long-lasting purple berries.
'Mend': leaves edged in white, turning reddish in bright light.

A. orlandiana (or-lan-dee-AH-na)
Upright rosette of green leaves with toothed margins and dark zebra-like bands beneath. Maroon spots develop on upper surfaces in bright light. Short flower cluster has yellow blossoms and scarlet bracts that last for months.
'Ensign' has spreading, stiffly pendulous leaves with creamy-white marginal bands. Foliage develops reddish spots in bright light.

SURFACE ROOTS — Alternating moist and dry conditions at the top of the soil mean that roots are rarely visible at the surface. Indoor plants grow like those outside, with roots protected by the top layer of soil which acts like a mulch. When soil is constantly moist, roots will grow close to the surface: some indoor plants prefer this non-stop moisture but for others the appearance of surface roots may signal saturated (or permanently dry) soil below.

Aeonium arboreum 'Atropurpureum'

Aeonium canariense

Aeschynanthus radicans

AEONIUM (ay-OH-ni-um)   **BL - WA - DS**

Easily grown succulents with single low-growing or clustered shrubby rosettes of fleshy leaves, spread 10-36" (25-90cm). Flowers late winter or spring. Branched clusters of tiny yellow, sometimes white or pink blossoms rise to 36" (90cm). Durable indoor plants; grow well on patio in warm climates. Grow in sandy indoor mix; repot infrequently. Propagate from stem cuttings (branching varieties), offsets that replace mature rosette after flowering, or seed.

MAINTENANCE Avoid direct scorching sun. Fertilize every month only while growing; none when dormant. Leafy rosettes tend to close and shrink in dormancy. Keep dormant plant cool, completely dry, and well lighted. Leaves wilt and rot with too much water. Dry brown spots indicate underwatering.

A. arboreum 'Atropurpureum' (ar-BOH-ree-um at-roh-pur-PEW-ree-um)
Black Tree Aeonium
Rosettes of 2-3" (5-8cm) fleshy coppery to deep purple leaves top branched stems. Flowers golden yellow. Shrubby growth to 36" (90cm).

A. canariense (ka-ne-ree-EN-see)
Canary Island Aeonium, Giant Velvet Rose, Velvet Rose
Single low rosette spreads to 30" (75cm). Soft, light green leaves 4-12" (10-30cm) long. Pale yellow flower cluster 12-18" (30-45cm) tall.

A. decorum (de-KOH-rum)
Copper Pinwheel
Shrub-like, branched plant with scaly stems and rosettes of glowing copper-tinted, red-edged leaves. Freely clustering. Spreads 18-30" (45-75cm). White flowers edged in pink.

AESCHYNANTHUS (ee-ski-NAN-thus)   **BL - WA - H - PD**
Basket Plant, Blushwort
A. radicans (RAD-i-kanz)
[*A. lobbianus* (lo-bi-AH-nus)]
Lipstick Vine
Trailing, epiphytic gesneriad characteristic tubular, lipstick-shaped blossoms in brilliant red, orange, or yellow. Dark green or white-variegated (**'Variegata'**) gleaming leaves borne in one plane on slender vines. Best in hanging baskets; smaller plants effective in pots. Can be grown on tree fern bark blocks in humid conditions. For containers, grow in acid soil (pH 6.0-7.0), using humusy or basic gesneriad mix. Repot infrequently. Fibrous roots. Propagate from stem cuttings.

AFTER FLOWERING, prune shoots to 6" (15cm) to encourage strong new growth. Water less often as growth slows. Flowering starts in spring after cool and dry resting period, continues into summer with 65°F (18°C) minimum nights. Light needed for flower development.

Agave americana

Agave angustifolia 'Marginata'

MAINTENANCE Avoid strong sun in summer and outdoors. Spray or mist with water to clean. Trim to shape. Fertilize every 3-6 weeks at half recommended strength while growing, every 6-12 weeks when growth slows in fall and winter. Cut off dying flowers, discolored foliage. Dry and cool air causes premature flower drop. Both fully dry and constantly wet soil cause root loss. Leach regularly to avoid damaging accumulation of soluble salts. White and brown dead areas on leaves can indicate sun-scorch. Check for spider mites and scale insects.

AGAVE (a-GAH-vee)   BL - WA - DS
Century Plant

Large tropical succulents have fleshy, sometimes spiny leaves. Slow growing; easy to grow. Tolerate periods of lower light and 50°F (10°C) temperatures. Stiff and formal, rarely reach flowering size when grown indoors. Fibrous roots. Plant in sandy indoor mix; repot infrequently. Propagate from offsets (suckers) in spring or summer.
MAINTENANCE Fertilize every month spring through summer only. Soil may remain dry for longer periods between waterings in winter. Constantly moist soil or poor drainage causes yellow leaves and root losses. Check for mealybugs and scale insects.

A. americana (a-me-ri-KAH-na)
Century Plant, Maguey, American Aloe
Broad rosette of spreading, arched grayish green leaves can grow as long as 5-8' (1.5-2.4m), width to 10" (25cm). Toothed or hooked edges; sharp spines at leaftips.

A. angustifolia 'Marginata' (an-goos-ti-FOH-li-a mar-ji-NAH-ta)
Variegated Caribbean Agave
White marginal bands on gray-green leaves that grow to 36" (90cm) long and 3-4" (8-10cm) wide. Compact, regular rosette has short stem. Freely suckering.

A. desmettiana (des-me-tee-AH-na))
[*A. miradorensis* (mi-ra-doh-REN-sis)]
Dwarf Century Plant
Rosette can grow to 5-6' (1.5-1.8m) in diameter, with graceful, often smooth-edged leaves that are deep green above, paler below. Red-brown spines at tips. Freely suckering.

A. victoriae-reginae (vik-TOH-ri-y-re-JEE-nay)
Queen Agave, Queen Victoria Agave
Small species. Stiff, blunt-tipped 6" (15cm) leaves in stemless rosette that grows to about 10" (25cm) high. Dark olive green leaves have crisp white margins. Rarely forms suckers.

Aglaonema 'Fransher'

Aglaonema 'Ramona'

Aglaonema 'Silver Queen'

Aglaonema 'Queen Julienne'

Aglaonema 'Silver King'

Aglaonema commutatum 'Emerald Beauty'

AGLAONEMA (ag-lay-oh-NEE-ma)   **LL/ML - WA - PD**

Tough, tolerant foliage plants with distinctive leaf colors and patterns. Leafy clusters spread slowly, become more open with age especially in very low light. Easy to grow. Use as contrast plant to brighten dull corner; in groups as accent or background; or as massed ground cover for interiorscape planting. Avoid drafty locations. Fleshy roots withstand occasional drought. Insignificant flowers develop when plants are rootbound. Grow in general indoor mix; repot infrequently. Propagate by division or from stem cuttings. Many named cultivars. Reported effective in tests to freshen or purify air (page 4).

MAINTENANCE Remove faded lower leaves. Fertilize every 2 months, or apply at half recommended strength every month. Leach regularly to avoid damaging accumulation of soluble salts.

Aglaonema cultivars:

A. 'Fransher': slender and colorful, with light gray markings on graceful leaves.

A. 'Malay Beauty' ['Pewter']: muted creamy markings. Height to 12-24" (30-60cm).

A. 'Parrot Jungle': silvery markings on dark green leaves.

A. 'Queen Julienne': modest silvery feathering on dark green leaves.

A. 'Ramona': compact cluster of silvered foliage.

A. 'Silver King': heavily silvered foliage clusters grow 24" (60cm) tall.

A. 'Silver Queen': silvery markings on gray-green leaves. Height about 18" (45cm).

Additional cultivars: **'Abidjan', 'B. J. Freeman', 'Bangkok', 'Lilian', 'Manila'** ['Manila Bay'], **'Pewter', 'San Remo', 'Silver Duke'.**

A. commutatum (ko-mew-TAH-tum)
Ribbon Aglaonema

Dark green, 12" (30cm) leaves have grayish markings along veins. Grows 2-3' (60-90cm) tall, spreads 18-24" (45-60cm).

'Emerald Beauty' ['Maria']: pale green markings on rich green foliage.
'Pseudobracteatum' (soo-doh-brak-tay-AH-tum) [*A. pseudobracteatum, A.* 'White Rajah']: showy pale yellow or white stems and crisply contrasting irregular leaf markings. Best in warm conditions.

A. costatum (kos-TAH-tum)
Spotted Evergreen

Broad, oval, deep green leaves spotted with white; central stripe also white. Grows slowly to 1-2' (30-60cm).

Aglaonema costatum

Allium schoenoprasum: chives

Aglaonema crispum

Alocasia Xamazonica

A. crispum (KRIS-pum)
[*A. roebelinii* (roh-be-LIN-ee-y)]
Pewter Plant, Painted Drop-tongue
Silvery variegations on mid-green leaves. Robust and showy, grows to 3-4' (0.9-1.2m). Tolerates very low light.

A. modestum (moh-DES-tum)
Chinese Evergreen
Shiny deep green leathery leaves rise to about 24" (60cm) on short clustering canes. Very easy. Tolerates very low light.

ALLIUM (AL-i-um) BL - CA - PD
A. schoenoprasum (shoh-noh-PRAY-sum)
Chives
Perennial herb. Cluster of cylindrical leaves grows rapidly 9-18" (23-45cm) tall. Snip onion-flavored foliage into salads, garnishes, gravies, and soups. Grow in general indoor mix. Tiny bulbs have short root systems. Propagate by division of existing plant, or from seed.
MAINTENANCE Cut off older shoots at soil level to encourage fresh new growth. Fertilize at half recommended strength every 2-4 weeks when growth is vigorous; every 4-8 weeks during winter. Remove flower stems to prolong leafy development. Divide or repot periodically.

ALOCASIA (a-loh-KAY-zi-a) LL/ML - WA - H - MS
Elephant's-ear Plant
Tropical foliage plant with big colorful, heart-shaped or arrow-like leaves on slender stems. Container or planter accent for large display or interiorscape in warm, humid, draft-free location. Best with warm nights, minimum 70°F (21°C). Grow in well-draining humusy indoor mix; for larger containers, add coarser humus like fir bark or chopped osmunda fibers; repot infrequently. Propagate by division of rhizomes, or from stem cuttings or seed.
MAINTENANCE Fertilize at half recommended strength every month when growing. Remove flowers to stimulate foliage development. When dormant, let soil become partly dry between waterings.

A. Xamazonica (a-ma-ZON-i-ka)
Robust growth, deep green foliage has showy white veins and undulating margins. Leaves 24" (60cm) long and 12" (30cm) wide.

A. sanderana (san-de-RAH-na)
[*A. sanderiana* (san-de-ree-AH-na)]
Triangular, 16" (40cm) arrowhead leaves are about 7" (18cm) wide with scalloped edges. Metallic dark green with silvery-gray veins, purple undersides.

Aloe arborescens

Aloe barbadensis (mature plant)

Aloe barbadensis (young plant)

Aloe nobilis

ALOE (AL-oh-ee) BL - WA - DS
Aloe (AL-oh)

Durable, easily grown succulents similar to but less fibrous and tough than *Agave*. Most are stemless basal leafy rosettes, some have branching stems. Slow growth; may flower indoors. Fibrous roots. Grow in sandy indoor mix; repot infrequently. Propagate by division, from offsets or stem cuttings when available.

MAINTENANCE Fertilize at half recommended strength every month in spring and summer; none in winter. Check for mealybugs.

A. arborescens (ar-boh-RES-enz)
Candelabra Aloe, Octopus Plant, Torch Plant
Upright stem grows 24-36" (60-90cm) and more, eventually branching to form 10-12' (3-3.6m) tree or shrub. Spreading rosette of bluish green fleshy leaves edged with yellow horny teeth. Mature leaves can grow 20" (50cm) long. Flowers in winter.

A. barbadensis (bar-ba-DEN-sis)
[*A. vera* (VEE-ra)]
Barbados Aloe, Curaçao Aloe, Medicinal Aloe, True Aloe
Stemless leafy clusters can spread 24-36" (60-90cm) or more, with leaves up to 24" (60cm) long. Young foliage is spotted or flecked white, older leaves edged with soft yellow spines. Clusters of yellow flowers rise to about 36" (90cm). Juice long known as effective soothing unguent for burns, sores, and cuts.

A. mitriformis (my-tri-FOR-mis)
Purple-crown, Purple-and-gold-crown
Dense rosettes of 8" (20cm) leaves with golden marginal teeth on sprawling stems. Red flowers.

A. nobilis (NOH-bi-lis)
Golden-tooth Aloe, Green-and-gold-crown
Big clusters of thick leaves have many sharp teeth along edges.

A. variegata (ve-ri-e-GAH-ta)
Tiger Aloe, Partridge-breast, Pheasant's-wings, Kanniedood Aloe
Stemless rosettes grow to 9" (23cm) with three ranks of fleshy foliage. Triangular blue-green leaves have striking white spots and crossbands, tough whitish margins. Offsets grow from active stolons, can form large clumps. Salmon-pink blossoms. Avoid strong direct sunlight.

ANANAS (AN-a-nas) BL - WA - PD
Sturdy bromeliad grows in rosette 2-4' (0.6-1.2m). Flowering stem bears dense cluster of blossoms above leaves, forms new leafy rosette or crown at top of fruit. Small, fleshy root system; plants rarely need repotting. Grow in porous, slightly acid bromeliad mix with sand.

Aloe variegata

Anethum graveolens: dill

Ananas comosus 'Variegatus'

Propagate in late spring and summer from offsets and leafy crown. AFTER FLOWERING, young plants grow at plant base and on flowering stem. When offsets have five or more well developed leaves, remove from mature parent plant. Let cut surfaces dry in air 24-48 hours before planting. Pot separately.

MAINTENANCE Mist every few days to provide more water for growth. Clean with gentle warm water spray. Fertilize every 1-2 months. Provide relative humidity 30% or more; brown leaf tips indicate dry air. Trim damaged, discolored parts. Check for scale insects, mealybugs, and basal rot. TO ROOT PINEAPPLE CROWN from store-bought fruit, cut or twist off just above flesh of fruit. Remove 10-15 basal leaves to reveal lower portion of stem. *To root in water:* Place in jar with water up to lowest remaining leaves. Add daily to maintain level; change water every few days to avoid decay. Roots grow in 7-10 days; plant in soil when about 1" (2.5cm) long. *To root in soil:* Dry in air 6-7 days. Plant in soil, firm well, and water thoroughly. Rooting hormone, applied to cut edge at planting time, inhibits decay and stimulates root growth.

A. bracteatus var. *striatus* (brak-tay-AH-tus stry-AH-tus)
Variegated Pineapple
Large rosette of spiny leaves with broad, creamy white, marginal stripes. Length about 36" (90cm), width 1½" (4cm). Showy red flower clusters. Fertilize sparingly.

A. comosus (ko-MOH-sus)
Pineapple
Rosette of stiff, arching, grayish to bronze-green foliage 20-40" (0.5-1.0m) high, with spiny tips and prickly edges. Violet flowers in dense head crowned by leafy tuft. Fruit aromatic with edible, seedless, yellow flesh. Commercial pineapple cultivars derived from this species.
'Variegatus' (ve-ri-e-GAH-tus), **Variegated Pineapple:** graceful, symmetrical rosette of ivory-yellow and green striped leaves. Bright light results in rose red tint. Pink flowers followed by pink fruit that rarely ripens, is doubtfully edible.

ANETHUM (a-NAY-thum)   BL - CA - MS
A. graveolens (gra-VEE-oh-lenz)
Dill
Aromatic annual herb grows rapidly to about 12" (30cm) indoors. Dill weed — stem, fine blue-green leaves, and yellow flowers — flavors salads, seafood, vegetables, meats, and sauces. Seeds have stronger flavor, are used in pickles, breads, soups. Start from seed or pot young plants in general indoor mix. Plants mature in 6-8 weeks.
MAINTENANCE Harvest foliage regularly to contain size. Fertilize at half recommended strength every 2-4 weeks when growing; every 4-8 weeks during winter. Wash with water to discourage spider mites.

Anthurium andraeanum

Anthurium 'Lady Jane'

Anthurium clarinervium

ANTHURIUM (an-THEW-ri-um) ML - WA - H - PD

Tropical foliage plants regularly produce unusual, long-lasting flowers. Big, smooth dark green or velvety leaves. Single waxy bract (spathe) reveals true flowers packed tightly on single spike (spadix). Many named cultivars. Container or planter accent, interiorscapes. Grow in well-draining humusy indoor mix; add coarser humus like fir bark or chopped osmunda fibers in larger containers. Leave space to add soil later as new fleshy roots grow from main stem. Propagate from stem cuttings or plantlets.

AFTER FLOWERING, remove faded flowers. Flowering continues with adequate humidity and diffused light.

MAINTENANCE Wash whole plants with plain tepid water or clean leaves with damp soft cloth. Fertilize at half recommended strength every month during active growth (spring through fall). Check for mealybugs and scale insects.

A. 'Lady Jane' ['Pink Princess']: slender, clear pink bracts curve open to reveal long, pink-tipped flower spikes; glossy dark green leaves.

Additional cultivar: **'Southern Blush'.**

A. andreanum hybrids (an-dree-AH-num)
Flamingo Flower
Long lasting heart-shaped flower bracts in white, ivory, yellow, orange, red, and pink. Dark green leaves.

A. clarinervium (kla-ri-NER-vi-um)
Hoja de Corazón
Compact species has distinctive dark green velvety foliage with clear silvery or ivory veins. Leaves form eye-catching accent, each about 5" (13cm) long and 4" (10cm) wide.

A. hookeri (HOO-ke-ry)
Birdsnest Anthurium
Unusually long, clustered, short-stemmed leaves form symmetrical green rosette, 24-36" (60-90cm) high. Short, small flowers. Prefers very high humidity of greenhouse or conservatory.

A. scherzeranum cultivars (skairt-ze-RAH-num)
[*A. scherzerianum*]
Flamingo Flower, Pigtail Anthurium, Pigtail Plant, Flame Plant
Compact, colorful cultivars flower in shades of red, pink, white, and yellow. Height about 16" (40cm).

Aphelandra squarrosa 'Silver Cloud'

Aphelandra chamissoniana

Aphelandra squarrosa

APHELANDRA (a-fe-LAN-dra)   ML/HL - WA - H- MS

Vigorous, upright evergreen tropical shrubs provide 1-2 months with colorful flowering bracts, summer to fall. Yellow blossoms extend from big cones of golden waxy bracts at stem top. Bright accents in flower, useful foliage addition without flowers. Grow in humusy indoor mix. Propagate from mature stem cuttings.

AFTER FLOWERING, cut off faded flower heads. Reduce watering frequency and stop fertilizing. Before growth resumes in spring, repot if needed; prune stems back to about 6" (15cm) to encourage strong new growth. As growth starts, increase water and fertilize.

MAINTENANCE Best with bright diffused light or partial shade. Clean leaves with moist soft cloth. Fertilize at half recommended strength every 2-4 weeks during growth and flowering. Leach regularly to avoid damaging buildup of soluble salts. Leaf-tips turn yellow in dry air, drafts. Leaves drop if soil is too wet or too dry. Check for mealybugs.

A. chamissoniana (ka-mi-soh-nee-AH-na)
Yellow Pagoda
Closely spaced, slender, 4-5" (10.0-12.5cm) leaves have silvery white bands along veins and midribs. Clear yellow flowers, green-tipped bracts. Prefers higher humidity than other aphelandras.

A. squarrosa cultivars (skwah-ROH-sa)
Zebra Plant, Saffron-spike
Dark green, glossy, ivory-veined leaves are 6-10" (15-25cm) long.
'Dania': compact habit, about 36" (90cm) high.
'Silver Cloud': silvery-cream midrib and veins.

LIGHT for indoor plants (page 6)
  LL - LOW LIGHT: performs well in low light conditions, or shade.
  ML - MODERATE LIGHT: performs well in part shade or diffused light.
  BL - BRIGHT LIGHT: performs well in full sun or bright indirect light.
HUMIDITY (page 7)
  H - Best with relative humidity 50% or more
TEMPERATURE (page 7)
  CA - COOL to AVERAGE TEMPERATURES: days 60-75°F (16-24°C), nights as cool as 45°F (7°C).
  WA - AVERAGE to WARM TEMPERATURES: days 70-80°F (21-27°C), nights 60-65°F (16-18°C).
WATERING (page 8)
  MS - Keep soil moist.
  PD - Let soil become partly dry between waterings.
  DS - Allow soil to dry out between thorough waterings.

Araucaria heterophylla

Ardisia crenata

ARAUCARIA (a-raw-KAH-ri-a)   ML - CA - PD
A. heterophylla (he-te-roh-FIL-a)
[*A. excelsa* (ek-SEL-sa)]
Norfolk Island Pine, Australian Pine, House Pine

Elegant, tolerant conifer thrives for many years in home conditions and interiorscape plantings. Easy to grow. Branches extend in horizontal tiers from woody trunk. Place where tree will not be damaged by traffic; broken branches do not grow back. Slow growth. Repot occasionally when tough fibrous roots fill container and/or to anchor taller tree, using general indoor mix; add fresh mix to surface in 9-10" (23-25cm) containers unless all soil needs to be replaced. Propagate by seed, or root top of damaged or old tree.

MAINTENANCE Fertilize at half recommended strength every 4-8 weeks spring through fall. Needle drop can result from sudden dry air, drafts, dry soil. Check for spider mites and mealybugs.

> Plants in high humidity conditions are especially vulnerable to bacterial and fungal infections. African Violets (*Saintpaulia*), with their close rosettes of thick fleshy leaves, are prime examples of plants that must be kept clean of dead and dying tissue.

ARDISIA (ar-DIS-i-a)   ML/BL - CA - MS/PD
A. crenata (kre-NAH-ta)
[*A. crenulata* (kre-new-LAH-ta)]
Coralberry, Spiceberry

Graceful shrub grows slowly to height and spread of about 36" (90cm) indoors. Gleaming dark green leathery leaves. Fragrant white or pink summer flowers. Bright coral waxy berries develop in winter, may persist six months. Attractive specimen or accent. Grow in well-draining general indoor mix. Fibrous roots. Repot if needed in early spring. Propagate from mature stem cuttings.

AFTER FLOWERING & FRUITING, trim off faded fruits. Prune plants back in late winter and keep soil dry until new growth starts. Then increase water and resume fertilizing. Trim to select strongest new shoots until flower buds develop.

MAINTENANCE Best with bright diffused light or partial shade. Keep soil moist during growth before flowering; reduce slightly at flowering, and allow partial drying during winter. Fertilize every 4-8 weeks in spring and summer. Leach regularly to avoid damaging accumulation of soluble salts. Check for spider mites.

Arecastrum romanzoffianum

Ariocarpus fissuratus

Artemisia dracunculus: tarragon

ARECASTRUM (a-re-KAST-rum)   ML - WA - PD
[Syagrus (sy-AH-grus)]
A. romanzoffianum (roh-man-zo-fee-AH-num)
[Syagrus romanzoffiana (roh-man-zo-fee-AH-na)]
Queen Palm
Subtropical feather palm with cluster of large arching or drooping foliage on straight gray-brown trunk. Leaves grow to 10-15' (3-4.5m) long, with narrow, shiny green leaflets. Mature plants flower; fruit edible. Grows quickly to 20-30' (6-9m), taller when planted outdoors. Allow space for natural, uncrowded growth. Tolerates some shade. Grow in rich, humusy palm mix. Propagate from seed.
MAINTENANCE Wipe leaves or wash with water to remove dust. Fertilize every month spring to fall, using a mixture containing 2-3% manganese. Trim damaged, discolored foliage. Check for spider mites.

ARIOCARPUS (a-ree-oh-KAR-pus)
Living-rock Cactus
A. fissuratus (fiss-ew-RAH-tus)   BL - WA/CA - DS
Living-rock, Star Cactus
Star-shaped flat succulent rosette grows very slowly to about 6" (15cm) across, 4" (10cm) high. Flattened stem covered with overlapping triangular leaf-like projections called tubercles. Horny, brownish green or gray surface with tufts of wool on tip of each fleshy tubercle. Pink flowers in fall, diameter about 1¾" (4.5cm). Unusual accent or specimen. Thickened root. Grow in dry cactus mix or well-draining sandy indoor mix; add limestone to reduce acidity. Propagate from seed.
MAINTENANCE Provide warm temperatures when growing, cool when dormant. Do not water during dormancy. Mist lightly with water in dry climates. Fertilize at half recommended strength every 2 months spring to summer. Rots caused by overwatering and excess humidity.

ARTEMISIA (ar-te-MIZ-i-a)   BL - CA - PD
A. dracunculus (dra-KUN-kew-lus)
Tarragon
Gray-green perennial herb grows to about 12" (30cm) indoors. Flavorful leaves used with seafood, meat, poultry, soups, salads, egg dishes, sauces, and pickles. Tiny flowers may not set seed. Grow in well-draining general indoor mix. Repot regularly to accommodate vigorous roots and creeping rhizomes. Propagate by division or from cuttings.
A. d. var. sativa (sa-TY-va), **French Tarragon:** flavor often preferred.
MAINTENANCE Harvest leaves and prune regularly to contain growth. Fertilize at half recommended strength every 2-4 weeks when growth is vigorous; every 4-8 weeks during winter. Wash with water to discourage spider mites.

Asparagus densiflorus 'Myers'

Asparagus macowanii

Asparagus densiflorus 'Sprengeri'

Asparagus setaceus

ASPARAGUS (as-PAH-ra-gus)   ML - CA - PD

Fast-growing fern-like perennials with spreading, upright, or climbing stems. Needles are modified branchlets called cladodes. Leaves
scale-like or spiny. Small greenish or white blossoms, red to purple
berries. Easy to grow. Prefer moderate climate, though tolerate wide
range of temperature and light conditions. Good for accent, specimen,
massed displays. Grow in well-draining general indoor mix; repot when
fleshy roots fill container. Propagate by division or from seed.
MAINTENANCE Trim stems to encourage bushiness. In spring, cut
back overgrown plants to soil level. Keep soil lightly moist until top
growth is established. Fertilize every 3-4 months, or apply at one-quarter recommended strength every 2 weeks. Fronds turn yellow in hot
sun. Check for spider mites and aphids. Sensitive to chemical sprays.

A. densiflorus cultivars (den-si-FLOH-rus)
'Myers', Foxtail Fern: stiff upright and spreading stems grow to 24"
(60cm), densely clothed with dark green needles, tapering to tips.
Durable. Best in moderate light, no direct sun.
'Sprengeri', Sprenger Asparagus, Emerald Fern, Emerald Feather:
wiry stems grow to 36" (90cm) long, arching and trailing, loosely
branched, covered with bright green fluffy needles. True leaves modified to tiny thorns. Good basket plant.

A. macowanii (ma-koh-WAH-nee-y)
Ming Fern
Upright, woody stems grow 2-6' (0.6-1.8m) high with short branch-
es. Bright green clusters of soft needles.

A. setaceus (se-TAY-see-us)
[*A. plumosus* (ploo-MOH-sus)]
Asparagus Fern, Lace Fern, Plumosa Fern
Long, climbing, wiry stems with flattened triangular clusters or fern-
like sprays of tiny needles. Small curved spines.

ASPIDISTRA (as-pi-DIS-tra)
A. elatior (e-LAH-ti-or)   LL/ML - CA/WA - PD
Barroom Plant, Cast-iron Plant
Tough, durable, easily-grown foliage plants tolerate neglect, polluted
air, very dark corners, too much and too little water, and hot and cold
temperatures. Clusters of glossy dark green leaves rise 2-3' (60-90cm).
Purple-brown flowers rise just above soil in spring. Good as accent,
specimen, or in group and massed displays; useful for spots where no
other plants will grow. Slow-growing. Grow in general indoor mix;
repot in spring when thick roots and rhizomes fill container. Propagate
by division.

Aspidistra elatior

Asplenium nidus

Asplenium bulbiferum

Asplenium daucifolium

'Variegata' (ve-ri-e-GAH-ta), **Variegated Cast-iron Plant:** uneven longitudinal striping in green and creamy-white. Less tolerant than green form. Keep on the dry side and fertilize sparingly; variegation less distinct in rich, moist soil.

MAINTENANCE In winter, let soil dry more between waterings. Clean with moist cloth or shower of tepid water. Trim off old and yellowed leaves. Fertilize at half recommended strength every 4-6 weeks spring through summer. Fluorides in soil or water can damage leaf margins.

ASPLENIUM (as-PLEE-ni-um) ML - WA - PD
Spleenwort

Epiphytic (tree-dwelling) ferns adapt well to containers and airy indoor conditions. Fronds vary from long shiny undulating ribbons to more typically fern-like divided leaves. Larger leaved forms are wide-spreading specimen or accent plants; others useful in terrariums, baskets, on pedestals, in groups. Sparse fibrous roots. Grow in shallow container like half-pot or azalea pot, or reduce soil depth with deep underlayer of broken clean pot. Plant in humus-rich fern mix; repot infrequently. Propagate by division or from plantlets.

MAINTENANCE In winter, let soil dry more between waterings. Benefits from moderate sunlight during colder weather. Protect from drafts. Spray gently with tepid water to remove dust from tender fronds.

Fertilize at one-quarter recommended strength every 4-6 weeks while growing. Leaf edges will spot brown if air is too cool or soil is too damp. Check for slugs and snails around ferns from outdoors. Sensitive to chemical sprays.

A. bulbiferum (bul-BIF-e-rum) **H**
Hen-and-chickens Fern, Mother Fern, Parsley Fern
Finely-divided fronds arch to height of 2' (60cm). New fernlets grow from small round buds on mature fronds; pin to moist soil, or detach and plant in enclosed container until well-rooted.

A. daucifolium (daw-ki-FOH-li-um) **H**
[*A. viviparum* (vi-VIP-a-rum)]
Mauritius Mother Fern
Miniature mother fern in dark green. New fernlets develop on mature fronds. Height 10-15" (25-38cm), spread 18-30" (45-75cm).

A. nidus (NEE-dus) **LL**
Bird's-nest Fern, Nest Fern
Spreading rosette of arched bright green fronds with dark stems surround circular rhizome, forming nest. New fronds spread from eggshaped coils, growing to 4' (1.2m) long and 8" (20cm) wide. Easy to grow. Best with relative humidity 30% or more; will grow in drier air than many ferns. Tolerates dry soil for short periods.

Beaucarnea recurvata

Begonia foliosa var. *miniata*

Begonia coccinea

Begonia X*hiemalis*

BEAUCARNEA (boh-KAR-nee-a)   ML/BL - CA/WA - PD
Bottle Ponytail
B. recurvata (ree-kur-VAH-ta)
[*Nolina recurvata* (noh-LY-na)]
Elephant-foot Tree, Ponytail
Succulent foliage plant has dark green leafy cluster arching or cascading from top of grayish wrinkled trunk-like stem. Long-lived, easy, adaptable. Narrow, tough leaves grow 3-5' (0.9-1.5m) long. Plant height 1-6' (0.3-1.8m). Rarely flowers and fruits during indoor cultivation. Good for mixed planting when young. Unusual conversation piece for low table or floor. Tolerates wide range of temperatures, from 40°F (5°C) to 100°F (38°C) or more. Swollen stem base is reservoir for water, so ponytail can withstand some drought. Very slow-growing. Small, fleshy root system. Grow in general indoor mix; repot and fertilize in spring to encourage growth. Propagate from offshoots or seed.
MAINTENANCE Wash with tepid water to remove dust. Fertilize every 3-4 months. Check for spider mites, mealybugs, and scale insects, especially if nearby plants have been infested.

BEGONIA (be-GOH-ni-a)   ML - WA - H - PD
Flowering and foliage plants for more humid though airy locations. Various types include *cane-type, hiemalis, rex, rhizomatous, semperflorens, shrubby*, and *tuberous*. May be short-lived. Grow as specimens and accents, in hanging baskets, as seasonal displays. Fibrous roots; some begonias have tubers or rhizomes. Grow in well-draining humusy indoor mix. Repot most begonias in early spring. Propagate from seed (semperflorens, tuberous), stem cuttings (cane-type, hiemalis, semperflorens, shrubby), tuber offsets (tuberous), rhizome sections (rex, rhizomatous), or leaf cuttings (rex).
MAINTENANCE Plant tops and soil surface should dry between waterings to avoid fungal rots. Pinch back excessively long growth; prune hard in spring for rapid new growth. Fertilize at half recommended strength every 4-6 weeks. Sensitive to waterlogging: roots drown, crown may rot. Leaves become limp if soil is too wet or too dry. Check for whitefly, aphids, mealybugs, spider mites, and powdery mildew.

B. coccinea cultivars (kok-SIN-ee-a)
Angel-wing Begonia
Cane-type plant with stems rising to 4' (1.2m). Narrow oval glossy green leaves. Abundant pendulous clusters of pink, coral, or red flowers in spring. Easy to grow.

Begonia masoniana

Begonia Rex-Cultorum hybrid

Begonia Semperflorens-Cultorum 'Charm'

Begonia Semperflorens-Cultorum hybrid

Begonia Tuberhybrida hybrid, Pendula group

B. foliosa (foh-lee-OH-sa)
Babylon Lace, Fernleaf Begonia
Shrub-like begonia has tiny leaves on arching, cascading stems that grow to 3' (90cm) long. Clusters of white, pink, or red flowers.
B. f. var. *miniata* (mi-ni-AH-ta) [*B. fuchsioides*], **Fuchsia Begonia, Corazón-de-Jesús:** red, fuchsia-like flowers.
'Rosea' (ROH-zee-a) [*B. floribunda*]: rose-pink flowers.

B. ✕*hiemalis* cultivars (hy-e-MAH-lis)   **CA**
Rieger Begonias, Winter-flowering Begonias
Bushy, compact hybrids with large, often double, colorful blossoms. Foliage green, bronze or red. After flowering, cut back and repot; water sparingly and do not fertilize until new growth is established.

B. masoniana (ma-soh-ni-AH-na)
Iron Cross Begonia
Rhizomatous foliage plant has shallow root system. Height 8-10" (20-25cm). Boldly marked, military-stiff bristly leaves.

B. Rex-Cultorum hybrids (REKS-cul-TOH-rum)
Rex Begonia
Rhizomatous foliage plant with shallow root system. Many variations of royal colors. Foliage mounds 12-18" (30-45cm) high. Tiny flowers.

B. Semperflorens-Cultorum hybrids (sem-per-FLOH-renz)   **BL**
Bedding Begonia, Wax Begonia, Busy Lizzie
Long-lasting yet delicate blossoms provide prolonged displays in sunny, airy locations. Green, red, bronze, or variegated foliage. Small plants mound to 6-12" (15-30cm). Easy plants for pot or basket; grow outdoors as annual bedding plant. After flowering, cut back and repot; water sparingly and do not fertilize until new growth is established.
'Charm', Variegated Wax Begonia: bright yellow and white markings on fresh green foliage; pink flowers.

B. Tuberhybrida hybrids (tew-ber-HYB-ri-da)   **CA**
Hybrid Tuberous Begonia
Seasonal flowering plant has lavish fresh green foliage and colorful blossoms. Plant in pot or basket. After flowering and as leaves die back, reduce watering frequency and stop fertilizing. Store dry tubers in or out of soil in frost-free, dark, dry place. Repot in late winter. Water well; place in moderate to bright light to encourage strong growth. When first leaves are fully expanded, resume monthly fertilizer applications. Several groups, including those with flowers shaped like camellias or carnations, on pendulous or upright stems.
Pendula group (PEN-dew-la), **Pendulous Begonia:** profuse flowers in bright, clear colors cluster on pendulous stems.

Billbergia 'Fantasia'

Billbergia nutans

Billbergia 'Muriel Waterman'

Billbergia pyramidalis

BILLBERGIA (bil-BER-ji-a) **BL/ML - WA - PD**

Slender, tubular leafy rosettes multiply to fill container. Dense flower clusters with colorful bracts. Easy accent plants. Tolerate shade with best form and color in brighter light. Grow in porous, slightly acid bromeliad mix. Propagate by division or from offsets.

AFTER FLOWERING, young plants, or offsets, grow at plant base. When one-third the size of the parent plant, remove offsets and plant.
MAINTENANCE Keep water in cup or funnel at all times. Mist foliage every few days to provide more water for growth. Clean with gentle spray of warm water. Fertilize at one-quarter recommended strength, applied to soil and cup every 4 weeks. Provide relative humidity 30% or more; brown leaf tips indicate dry air. Trim damaged, discolored parts. Check for scale insects, mealybugs, and basal rot.

B. 'Fantasia': broad green leaves, marbled with ivory and rose, form tight rosette. Flower cluster has crimson bracts and violet blossoms.

B. 'Muriel Waterman': close rosette of plum-colored leaves with silvery gray banding. Pink flower bracts, dark blue flowers.

B. nutans (NEW-tanz)
Friendship Plant, Queen's-tears
Slender olive-green leaves cluster gracefully, turn reddish in full sun. Weeping flowers cluster on long pink stems.

B. pyramidalis (pi-ra-mi-DAH-lis)
Foolproof Plant, Summer Torch
Stiff, broad green leaves grow to about 24" (60cm) long in close, spreading rosette. Bright orange-red 4" (10cm) flower spike.
'Kyoto': white-margined foliage. Height 18-24" (45-60cm).

BORZICACTUS (bor-zi-KAK-tus) **BL - WA/CA - DS**
[*Oreocereus* (o-ree-oh-SEE-ree-us)]
Rounded to columnar spiny cacti with soft, hair-like bristles that grow more densely in brighter light. Accent for sunny windowsill. Slow growing. Plant in dry cactus mix or well-draining sandy indoor mix.
MAINTENANCE Provide warm temperatures when growing and cool when dormant, usually in winter. Water sparingly during dormancy. Fertilize at half recommended strength every 2 months in spring and summer. Rotting can result from overwatering and excess humidity.

B. celsianus (sel-see-AH-nus)
Old-man-of-the-mountains, South American Old-man
Stout yellow-brown spines grow as long as 3" (7.5cm).

B. trollii (TROL-ee-y)
Old-man-of-the-Andes
Dense silvery bristles cover green stem and slightly curved spines.

Borzicactus celsianus   *Borzicactus trollii*

Bougainvillea 'Raspberry Ice'

Brassaia (Schefflera) actinophylla

BOUGAINVILLEA (boo-gan-VIL-ee-a)   **BL - WA - H - DS**
Paper Flower

Flowering vine with woody, spiny stems. Many named cultivars. Profuse blossoms with colorful papery bracts in pinks, purples, white. Light green or variegated foliage. Bright, airy location indoors or on patio. Vine can be pruned and trained to standard form. Move outdoors to partial shade during summer. Year-round, sunloving outdoor plant in warmer climates. Loose, thin, fibrous root system. Grow in general indoor mix; topdress with fresh mix in spring rather than repot. Propagate from soft cuttings or seed.

AFTER FLOWERING, leaves fall for brief dormant period. New growth develops immediately in ideal conditions. Trim, prune at this time. Reduce watering and fertilizing, increasing again with new growth. Flowering resumes with sufficient light.

MAINTENANCE Prune to shape. Support long stems on stakes or frame. Cut off unwanted stems at soil level to encourage strong new growth. Fertilize at half recommended strength every 2-4 weeks spring and summer, every 4-8 weeks in winter depending on growth rate. Survives relative humidity lower than 50% with reduced flowering and less leafy development. Leaf drop results from root disturbance (such as repotting). Check for scale insects, and for rots and powdery mildew that can result from too much water on stems and leaves.

BRASSAIA (bra-SAY-a)   **ML/BL - WA - PD**
B. actinophylla

[*Schefflera actinophylla* (shef-LEE-ra)] (Also page 112)

Schefflera, Australian or **Queensland Umbrella Tree, Octopus Tree, Starleaf**

Handsome, durable foliage plant. Leaves palmately divided, umbrella-like; glossy green leaflets 4-12" (10-30cm) long. The taller the tree, the larger the leaflets. Height 6-12' (1.8-3.6m) or more in containers. Width varies; allow space for natural spread. Specimen for low table, floor. Useful in public buildings, entranceways, hallways. Move outdoors in summer, or plant in sheltered location in warmer climates. Tolerates cooler nights, down to 45°F (7°C). Thin spindly growth in low light. Fast-growing. Grow in general indoor mix; repot as needed. Propagate by air-layering or from mainstem cuttings.

MAINTENANCE In winter, let soil dry more between waterings. Place plant away from direct scorching sun. Cut back longest stem(s) or reduce stem length to contain size. Wipe with moist cloth to remove dust. Spray or wash to discourage spider mites. Fertilize at half recommended strength every 4-8 weeks. Good air circulation ensures rapid drying of foliage, avoids rots in humid conditions. Lower leaves drop with insufficient light. Leaf yellowing and burn results from cold drafts. Check for spider mites and scale insects.

Browallia speciosa

Caladium ×hortulanum 'Fannie Munson'

Caladium ×hortulanum 'Frieda Hemple'

Caladium ×hortulanum 'Candidum'

BROWALLIA (broh-WAH-lee-a)   **BL - WA - H- PD**
Bush Violet
B. speciosa cultivars (spee-si-OH-sa)
Flowering plant for bright humid locations. Spreading, trailing stems can be pruned and staked. Mounds 1-2' (30-60cm) high. Large flowers, to 2" (5cm) across, in vivid blues, purple, or white. Blossoms produced all year with sufficient light. Oval leaves to 4" (10cm) long. Graceful hanging basket; place pot on table or pedestal. Use in shaded location on porch, outdoors in summer or longer in warm climate. Grow in humusy indoor mix; repot in early summer. Propagate from seed or mature stem cuttings. Several named cultivars.
'Alba': white flowers.
'Major', **Sapphire Flower:** large blue flowers.
AFTER FLOWERING, prune as desired. Reduce watering and fertilizing, increasing again with new growth. Flowering resumes with sufficient light.
MAINTENANCE Fertilize at half recommended strength every 2-4 weeks spring and summer, every 4-8 weeks if flowering continues through fall and winter. Leaf scorch results from dry air or draft. Check for whitefly.

CALADIUM (ka-LAY-di-um)   **ML - WA - H - PD**
Elephant's-ear, Angel-wings
C. ×***hortulanum*** cultivars (hor-tew-LAH-num)
Fancy-leaved Caladium
Colorful, tropical foliage with big wafer-thin leaves. Height 2-4' (0.6-1.2m). Cultivars offer showy variations with green, white, pink, and red tones. Short-term container plants. Fast growing. Plant in well-draining humusy indoor mix. Propagate by division of dormant tubers.
MAINTENANCE Mist with water every few days when natural humidity is lower than 50 percent. Fertilize at half recommended rate every 2-3 weeks while growing. Check for whitefly. Reduce watering and stop fertilizing as leaves die. Store dry tubers at about 70°F (21°C). Repot as needed in late winter. Water well once. Growth starts at 75-85°F (21-29°C). Resume watering and fertilization as leaves expand.

CALATHEA (ka-LAY-thee-a)   **ML - WA - H - MS/PD**
Tropical foliage plants with variously striped and colored leaves. Clusters of leaves rise from rhizome. Tiny flowers. Showy specimen or accent plants for table, hanging basket, large terrarium, plant groups, interiorscape. Grow with shade outdoors in warm, humid climates. Plant in humusy indoor mix. Propagate by division.
MAINTENANCE Best with night temperature above 65°F (18°C). In winter let soil become partly dry between waterings. Pinch back leggy

Calathea concinna

Calathea zebrina

Calathea roseopicta

Calceolaria

growth and unwanted stems. Clean with gentle spray of tepid water. Fertilize at half recommended strength every 4-8 weeks. Leach regularly to avoid salts damage to sensitive fibrous roots. Trim off damaged and dead leaves. Fluorides in soil or water cause leaf margin damage.

C. concinna (kon-SIN-a)
Glossy gray-green leaves have precise dark green bands and margins.

C. makoyana (ma-koy-AH-na)
Peacock Plant, Cathedral Plant
Upright foliage on long stems; height 2-3" (60-90cm). Distinctive rounded markings on paper-thin leaves; silvery-olive and cream feathering on upper surfaces, cream with pink or purple on undersides.

C. ornata (or-NAH-ta)
Rich green leaves with purplish red reverse; pink becoming white lines mark veins. Leaves 2-3' (60-90cm) long; plant grows 3-4' (0.6-1.2m).
'Sanderana' (san-de-RAH-na): showy plant, broader glossy leaves.

C. picturata **'Vandenheckei'** (pik-tew-RAH-ta van-den-HEK-ee-y)
Elliptical leaves dark green with feathery white central and marginal bands, purple undersides.
C. p. **'Argentea'** (ar-JEN-tee-a): greenish-white upper leaf surface has dark green border.

C. roseopicta (roh-zee-oh-PIK-ta)
Compact plant grows to 8" (20cm). Dark green foliage marked with bright red and silvery-pink; red midribs.

C. rotundifolia **'Fasciata'** (roh-tun-di-FOH-li-a fa-see-AH-ta)
Silvery-white bands on rounded leaves. Height 12" (30cm).

C. zebrina (zee-BRY-na)
Zebra Plant
Bold, vigorous, compact plant grows to 1-3' (30-90cm). Velvety green leaves with pale midribs and veins; purplish-red undersides.

CALCEOLARIA (kal-see-oh-LAH-ri-a)   BL/ML - CA - PD
Pocketbook Plant, Pouch Flower, Slipper Flower
Short-term flowering plants usually available in spring. Pouch or slipper-shaped flowers in many brilliant and decorated hues cluster above large, slightly puckered leaves. Specimen or accent; mass for effective display. Grow with shade outdoors in warmer climates. Indoors, locate with bright indirect light or partial shade. Best with relative humidity 30% or more. Cooler nights prolong flowering. No fertilizer needed while in flower. Reduce watering frequency as flowers and leaves fade. Tender perennial best treated as an annual in containers. Grown from seed.

Caryota mitis

Carissa grandiflora 'Emerald Blanket'

Catharanthus roseus

CARISSA (ka-RIS-a)   BL - CA - PD
C. grandiflora 'Emerald Blanket' (gran-di-FLOH-ra)
Natal Plum
Spreading, shrubby, foliage plant with fragrant white blossoms and red plum-like fruits. Glossy evergreen leaves. Tolerates short periods of moderate to low light. Fibrous roots. Plant in general indoor mix. Repot infrequently. Propagate from stem cuttings.
MAINTENANCE In winter, let soil dry more between waterings. Prune to control size. Clean with gentle spray of water. Fertilize every 2-3 months spring through fall. New growth becomes spindly after prolonged exposure to low light. Check for scale insects and aphids.

CARYOTA (ka-ree-OH-ta)   BL/ML - WA - MS/PD
Fishtail Palm
C. mitis (MEE-tis)
Burmese Fishtail Palm, Clustered Fishtail Palm, Tufted Fishtail Palm
Clustering tropical feather palm with unique fan-shaped leaflets. Light green foliage. Grows slowly, height reaches 20-25' (6.0-7.5m) in sheltered, frost-free outdoor planting. Ideal container specimen for table or floor; small to medium interiorscape item. Tolerates shade. Prefers humid climate though tolerates dry air. Grow in well-draining, rich,

humusy palm mix. Propagate by division, seed.
MAINTENANCE In winter, let soil become partly dry between waterings. Wipe leaves or wash with water to remove dust. If possible, move to shaded outdoor position during warm months. Fertilize every month spring through fall. Trim damaged and discolored foliage. Check for spider mites and scale insects.

CATHARANTHUS (ka-tha-RAN-thus)   BL - WA - PD/DS
C. roseus selections (ROH-zee-us)
Madagascar Periwinkle, Rose Periwinkle
Seasonal flowering plants for bright conditions indoors and out. Perennial usually grown as annual. Smooth green foliage topped by phlox-like blossoms in rose, pink, pure white, or white with rose-red eye. Height 12-24" (30-60cm). Colorful summer addition for indoor and outdoor displays. Tolerates drought and outdoor temperatures of 90°F (32°C) and more. Grows rapidly from seed or cuttings. Plant in sandy indoor mix.
AFTER FLOWERING, trim off dead blossoms and prune back stems to shape plant. Let soil dry out between waterings until vigorous growth resumes in early spring. Fertilize at half recommended rate every 4-6 weeks during growth. Pinch tips as needed to encourage bushiness.
MAINTENANCE Check for whitefly and scale insects.

Cattleya 'Susan Strambland'

Cattleya 'Apollo'

Cephalocereus senilis

CATTLEYA (KAT-lee-a) BL - WA - H - DS
Queen of Orchids

Showy, tropical orchids have long-lasting, colorful, 4-6" (10-15cm) summer flowers. Light green, leathery, strap-like leaves rise in clusters from swollen stems or pseudobulbs. Grow with shade outdoors in summer. Epiphytic: mount to hang in humid greenhouse climate. For indoor containers use well-draining, moisture retaining mix containing both fibrous and water-holding materials: osmunda, coarsely shredded fir bark, redwood chips, or small pumice stones, with coarse peat moss and/or perlite. Or use ready-made epiphytic orchid mix. Fleshy roots with pale outer layer. Repot in spring every few years to renew soil. Propagate by division into smaller clusters, each with three or more pseudobulbs.

AFTER FLOWERING, reduce watering and fertilizing frequency while *Cattleya* rests in winter. When new growth starts, resume regular applications. Flowers develop with adequate light and humidity.

MAINTENANCE Avoid direct scorching sun in summer. While growing, water thoroughly as soon as soil is dry. Fertilize every 2-4 weeks while growing. Root rot results from poor drainage, overwatering. Dark leaves and soft new growth result from insufficient light. Check for slugs and snails on orchids moved in from outdoors, and indoors for spider mites, scale insects, mealybugs, rots, and leafspot.

CEPHALOCEREUS (se-fa-loh-SEE-ree-us) BL - WA/CA - DS
C. senilis (se-NEE-lis)
Old-man Cactus

Upright cylindrical cactus has single ribbed gray-green stem covered with clumps of grayish white hairs or bristles that elongate to about 12" (30cm). Yellow spines. Height 2-10' (0.6-3.0m) and diameter 4-10" (10-25cm) when grown in container. Flowers after several years; 2" (5cm) rose-colored blossoms open at night in spring. Specimen or accent for windowsill, cactus group. Fire retardant ground cover outdoors, spaced 6-12" (15-20cm) apart. Slow growing. Thickened, fibrous roots. Grow in well-draining sandy indoor mix; add limestone to reduce acidity. Propagate from seed or cuttings.

MAINTENANCE Provide warm temperatures when growing and cool when dormant, usually in winter. Water sparingly during dormancy. Fertilize at half recommended strength every 2 months in spring and summer. Rotting can result from overwatering and excess humidity.

TEMPERATURE (page 7)
CA - COOL to AVERAGE TEMPERATURES: days 60-75°F (16-24°C), nights as cool as 45°F (7°C).
WA - AVERAGE to WARM TEMPERATURES: days 70-80°F (21-27°C), nights 60-65°F (16-18°C).

Cereus peruvianus

Ceropegia woodii

Chamaecereus silvestri

CEREUS (SEE-ree-us) BL/ML - WA/CA - DS
C. peruvianus (pe-roo-vee-AH-nus)
Peruvian Apple, Apple Cactus, Column Cactus
Upright, branching, deeply ribbed blue-green cactus has short golden spines. White flowers 4" (10cm) across, about 6" (15cm) long, open at night in summer. Height 2-5' (0.6-1.5m) or more. Very tolerant; easy to grow. Fibrous roots. Grow in well-draining sandy indoor mix.
'Monstrosus', Giant Club, Curiosity Plant: smaller and slower-growing form with multiple contorted, crested stems.
MAINTENANCE Provide warm temperatures when growing and cool when dormant, usually in winter. Water sparingly during dormancy. Fertilize at half recommended strength every 2 months in spring and summer. Rotting can result from overwatering and excess humidity.

CEROPEGIA (se-roh-PEE-jee-a) BL - CA - DS/PD
C. woodii (WUD-ee-y)
Rosary Vine, Hearts Entangled, String-of-Hearts
Trailing succulent vine has heart-shaped leaves and swellings or tubercles along stems. Easily grown basket plant hangs 36" (90cm) or more. Foliage dark bluish green with distinctive silvery markings, purple undersides. Small tubular pinkish green flowers from spring to fall.

Tolerates dry conditions. Grow in well-draining, humusy indoor mix. Propagate from stem cuttings that include tubercles.
MAINTENANCE Best in bright indirect light; avoid direct sun especially in summer. During winter let soil become dry between waterings. Overwatering weakens vigor. Prefers cool nights at about 50°F (10°C) though tolerates warmer conditions. Cut back sparse, straggly, overlong stems. Fertilize at half recommended strength every 2-4 weeks, less often in winter. Check for mealybugs.

CHAMAECEREUS (ka-me-SEE-ree-us) BL - WA/CA - DS
C. silvestri (sil-VES-tree)
[*Echinopsis chamaecereus* (e-ki-NOP-sis)]
Peanut Cactus
Low-growing cactus has clustered stems with soft white spines. Overall height about 4" (10cm). Flowers orange-scarlet, about 3" (7.5cm) long, freely produced after long, dry, cool rest in winter. Shallow, wide container accommodates spreading peanut-like stems. Grow in well-draining sandy indoor mix. Propagate from sections of stem or stem cuttings.
MAINTENANCE Provide warm temperatures when growing and cool when dormant, usually in winter. Water sparingly during dormancy. Fertilize at half recommended strength every 2 months in spring and summer. Rotting can result from overwatering and excess humidity.

Chamaedorea elegans

Chamaedorea erumpens

Chlorophytum comosum 'Variegatum'

CHAMAEDOREA (ka-mee-DOH-ree-a) **ML/LL - WA - MS/PD**

Clustering or single stem tropical feather palms. Slow growing, long lived. Prefer humid climate though tolerate dry air. Avoid drafts. Grow in well-draining rich, humusy palm mix, or general indoor mix. MAINTENANCE Keep soil slightly moist. In winter, let soil become partly dry. Fertilize every month spring to fall. Fluorides in soil or water cause leaflet margin damage. Check for spider mites, scale insects, and leaf spot disease.

C. elegans (EL-e-ganz)
Good-luck Palm, Parlor Palm, Neanthe Bella Palm
Easy palm for small pots. Mature height 3-6' (0.9-1.8m). Single stem, often planted several in a pot. Tolerates crowding in well-draining soil.

C. erumpens (e-RUM-penz)
Bamboo Palm
Clustering. Grows to 4-5' (1.2-1.5m). Short, broad, curving leaflets. Reported effective in tests to freshen or purify air (page 4).

C. seifrizii (see-FRIZ-ee-y)
Reed Palm, Grass-leaved Parlor Palm
Clustering species with slender cane-like stems and long, narrow leaflets. Height to 8-10' (2.4-3.0m). Tolerates short periods of sun.

C. 'Florida Hybrid': columnar palm grows to 15' (4.5m). Glossy green leaflets; tolerates low light.

CHLOROPHYTUM (klo-roh-FY-tum) **ML - CA - PD/DS**

C. comosum (koh-MOH-sum)
Spider Plant, Green Spider Plant, Ribbon Plant
Durable foliage plant with arching, spreading green leaves. Developing plantlets cluster on pendulous branching stolons, can remain on parent plant for years. Flowering and plantlets stimulated by short days (long nights). Easily grown basket plant; tolerates drought, heat, cold. Fleshy tuberous roots. Grows rapidly. Repot before roots burst small containers, using general indoor mix without perlite; add limestone to reduce acidity. Propagate by division or from plantlets. Reported effective in tests to freshen or purify air (page 4).
'Picturatum': central creamy stripe on 12" (30cm) leaves.
'Variegatum', **Variegated Spider Plant:** white edged foliage.
'Vittatum', **Spider Plant:** upright, arching leaves to 16" (40cm) long.
MAINTENANCE Supply plenty of water when growing vigorously, less during winter. Wash with spray of tepid water. Fertilize every 4-8 weeks. Foliage scalds in direct hot sun. Leach regularly to avoid damaging accumulation of soluble salts. Fluorides in soil or water cause leaf tip damage. Check for whitefly, spider mites, scale insects.

Chrysalidocarpus lutescens

Chrysanthemum X*morifolium*

Chrysanthemum X*morifolium*

CHRYSALIDOCARPUS (kri-sa-li-doh-KAR-pus)

ML/BL - WA - MS/PD

Clustering, tropical feather palms. Prefers warmer indoor climate, away from full sun and cold drafts. Repot young groups as needed every 2-3 years in well-draining, rich, humusy palm mix. Propagate by division, seed.

MAINTENANCE In winter, let soil become partly dry between waterings. Wipe leaves or wash with water to remove dust. Fertilize every month spring through fall. Trim damaged and discolored foliage. Check for spider mites, mealybugs, and scale insects.

C. cabadae (KAB-a-dee)
Larger palm for malls, large-scale interiorscapes. Clustering, bamboo-like stems, height to 20-30' (6-9m).

C. lutescens (loo-TES-enz)
[*Areca lutescens* (a-REE-ka)]
Areca Palm, Bamboo Palm, Cane Palm, Yellow Butterfly Palm
Slow growth, expanding clusters with arching fronds. Small sizes in dish gardens, larger groups for table, floor accents, interiorscapes. Can reach 15-20' (4.5-6.0m) indoors. Fluorides in soil or water may cause leaflet margin damage.

CHRYSANTHEMUM (kri-SAN-the-mum)　　**BL - CA - PD**
C. X*morifolium* cultivars (mo-ri-FOH-li-um)
[*Dendranthema* X*grandiflorum* (den-DRAN-the-ma)]
Pot Chrysanthemum

Flowering plants for short term display. May be reflowered or grown outdoors, depending on climate and variety. Tolerate low light for short periods. Many colors and flower forms. Grow in well-draining general indoor mix. Propagate by division or from stem tip cuttings. Reported effective in tests to freshen or purify air (page 4).

AFTER FLOWERING, gradually reduce watering frequency as leaves die down. In winter, keep resting plant in cool dark place with barely damp soil until spring. Cut stems back to 2-4" (5-10cm), place in bright location indoors or plant out in sun or part shade. Water well. When new growth starts, fertilize every 2-4 weeks. Prune and pinch to shape until midsummer. Chrysanthemums flower naturally as nights get longer. Tender varieties may not survive winter outdoors. Pot mums often grow taller in home conditions than in commercial production.

MAINTENANCE Flowers last longest with bright indirect light and cool indoor nights. Do not fertilize while in flower. Overwatering and poor drainage result in wilting flowers, yellowing leaves. Check for whitefly, aphids, thrips, mealybugs, spider mites; avoid chemical treatments while in flower.

Cissus rhombifolia

XCitrofortunella mitis

CISSUS (SIS-us)   ML - WA - PD
Grape Ivy, Treebine Ivy
Long-lived foliage vines trail or climb. Flexible, woody stems. Tolerant of low light, dry air, cool nights. Repot infrequently, using general or humusy indoor mix. Propagate from stem cuttings.
MAINTENANCE   In winter, let soil dry between waterings. Pinch shoots to encourage bushiness. Clean with gentle spray of tepid water. Fertilize at half recommended strength every 4-8 weeks in spring and summer. Leach regularly to avoid damaging accumulation of soluble salts. Leaves sparse in poor light. Check for mealybugs, spider mites.

C. antarctica (an-TARK-ti-ka)
Kangaroo Ivy
Vigorous climbing vine for trellis, screen, hanging basket. Medium green, 2-3" (5.0-7.5cm) oval, tooth-edged leaves.

C. rhombifolia (rom-bi-FOH-li-a)
Grape Ivy, Venezuela Treebine
One of best indoor foliage basket vines. Dark, glossy green, 3-part leaves. Stems, lower veins have reddish hairs. Easy to grow.
'Ellen Danica', Oak-leaf Grape Ivy: leaflets lobed like oak leaves. Darker green, more compact.
'Fionia': slow-growing, with thick, shiny, lobed leaves.
'Mandaiana', Bold Grape Ivy: larger leaves, compact, upright habit.

X CITROFORTUNELLA (sit-roh-for-tew-NEL-a)
and CITRUS (SIT-rus)   BL - CA - H - PD
Leafy shrubs and small trees with fragrant blossoms and fruit. Specimen or accent plants for containers, interiorscape plantings. Move outdoors during summer. Slow growing. Fibrous roots. Repot infrequently, using acid, humusy indoor mix. Propagate from soft stem cuttings.
AFTER FLOWERING and fruiting, trim to shape plant. Water and fertilize regularly while new growth is made. Let soil dry longer between waterings during winter and when less-than-bright light slows growth. Flowers and fruits develop only in brightly lighted indoor conditions.
MAINTENANCE   Prune to desired shape and size. Clean with gentle spray of tepid water. Fertilize every 2 months with food for acid-loving plants. Leach regularly to avoid damaging buildup of soluble salts. Leaves turn yellow in alkaline soil conditions and/or with iron deficiency; add aluminum sulfate and chelated iron. Flower, fruit, leaf drop result from high salts or soil that is too wet or too dry. Check for whitefly, scale insects, spider mites, mealybugs.

X Citrofortunella mitis (MEE-tis)
[XC. microcarpa (my-kroh-KAR-pa), Citrus mitis]
Calamondin, Panama Orange
Miniature orange tree about 24" (60cm) high. Pinch stem tips to encourage spread. Tiny fruits edible though bitter.

Cleistocactus strausii

Clivia miniata

CLEISTOCACTUS (kly-stoh-KAK-tus)   BL - WA/CA - DS
C. strausii (STROW-see-y)
Silver-torch

Slender, cylindrical, light green cactus has many soft white bristles and yellow spines. Fast growing; reaches about 5' (1.5m) in 5 years. Branching upright habit; height to about 10' (3m) . Many tubular red flowers on specimens at least 2' (60cm) tall. Fibrous roots. Grow in well-draining sandy indoor mix. Propagate from stem cuttings or seed. MAINTENANCE Provide warm temperatures when growing and cool when dormant, usually in winter. Water sparingly during dormancy. Fertilize at half recommended strength every 2 months in spring and summer. Rotting can result from overwatering and excess humidity.

CLIVIA (KLY-vi-a)   ML - WA - PD
Kaffir Lily
C. miniata cultivars and hybrids (mi-ni-AH-ta)

Wide, strap-like, dark green leaves contrast with clusters of yellow, red, or orange flowers. Red fruits. Leaves 12-18" (30-45cm) long; flowering stems rise to about 15" (38cm). Flowers in late winter; best when rootbound. Fleshy, tuberous roots. Repot infrequently, using general indoor mix. Propagate by division in spring after flowering.

AFTER FLOWERING, continue to water and fertilize while new leaves develop. Trim off older, discolored foliage and dying flower stems. In fall and winter, stop fertilizing and let soil become dry between waterings. As new growth begins, increase watering frequency and resume fertilizer applications.
MAINTENANCE Best with minimum temperatures above 60°F (16°C). Water often to supply plants' needs during active growth. Clean with spray of tepid water or wipe leaves with moist soft cloth. Fertilize every month late winter through summer. Check for mealybugs.

CODIAEUM (koh-dee-Y-um)   BL/ML - WA - PD
C. variegatum cultivars (ve-ri-e-GAH-tum)
Croton, Variegated Laurel

Colorful foliage for bright, humid yet airy locations. Shrubs grow to height and spread of 2-4' (0.6-1.2m). Glossy, leathery leaves have diverse shapes, 12-18" (30-45cm) long, variegated with red, pink, yellow, orange, green. Best color develops with bright indirect light and humid air. Individual accent or specimen plants, or massed in group planting, interiorscapes. Grow in semi-shade outdoors in warmer climates. Fibrous roots. Repot every few years, using general indoor mix. Propagate by air layering or from cuttings. Many named cultivars.

Codiaeum variegatum

Coffea arabica

Codiaeum variegatum

Coleus Xhybridus

MAINTENANCE Best with bright light during winter, diffused light at other times. Pinch to encourage branching. Clean by wiping leaves with moist soft cloth or with gentle spray of tepid water. Fertilize every 1-2 months. Provide relative humidity 30% or more. Leaf drop can result from dry air, drafts, and/or dry soil. Check for scale insects, spider mites, mealybugs.

COFFEA (KOF-ee-a) ML/BL - WA - PD
C. arabica (a-RAB-i-ka)
Coffee Plant

Small, slender evergreen shrub with smooth foliage. Grows to about 35" (90cm). Fragrant flowers and red fruit may develop indoors on older plants. Specimen for table, floor; leafy contrast for group planting, interiorscape. Tolerates as cool as 50°F (10°C) for short periods. Fast growing. Fibrous roots. Plant in general indoor mix. Propagate from stem cuttings.

MAINTENANCE Water before leaves wilt to avoid permanent damage. In winter, let soil dry more between waterings. Prune to desired shape and size. Wash with gentle spray of tepid water. Fertilize every 1-2 months spring through summer. Provide relative humidity 30% or more when flowering. Leaf drop results from soil that is too wet or too dry.

COLEUS (KOH-lee-us) BL - WA - MS
Painted Leaves, Flame Nettle
C. X *hybridus* (HYB-ri-dus)
[*C. blumei, Solenostemon scutellarioides*]

Tropical foliage plants with brilliantly colored leaves. Often grown as annuals for seasonal displays indoors and out. Specimen or group plants for pots, planters, baskets. Easy; fast growing. Fibrous roots. Plant in well-draining humusy indoor mix. Propagate from seed or stem cuttings.

MAINTENANCE Best with minimum temperatures above 60°F (16°C) and with relative humidity 30% or more. Discard drainage water. Locate in strong indirect light; direct sun scorches tender foliage. Pinch tips to retain bushy habit. Remove flowering spikes to maintain compact leafy growth. If stems become leggy during winter, cut back in early spring. Fertilize at half recommended strength every 3-6 weeks spring through fall. Check for spider mites, mealybugs, whitefly, scale insects, and (outdoors) caterpillars and slugs.

TO LEACH PLANTS — Water well four or five times in succession, discarding all drainage water. For a more thorough leaching, saturate the soil by immersing the whole container almost to its brim; leave to soak for 10-15 minutes; remove, and allow soil to drain. Repeat several times.

Columnea 'Chocolate Soldier'

Columnea 'Great Horned'

Cordyline terminalis 'Kiwi'

Columnea 'Early Bird'

Columnea gloriosa

Cordyline terminalis 'Red Sister'

COLUMNEA (ko-LUM-nee-a)

BL - WA - H - PD

Trailing or shrubby epiphytic gesnariads offer range of leaf size and flower color for baskets. Best with high humidity yet tolerate drier climate. Grow in acid soil (pH 6.0-7.0), using humusy or basic gesneriad mix. Repot infrequently. Propagate from stem cuttings, by division. AFTER FLOWERING, trim more vigorous plants to desired shape and size. Water less often as growth slows, and maintain at lower temperatures until growth resumes in spring. Flower buds form in strong light after cooler and drier resting period.

MAINTENANCE Shade from strong sun. Avoid extreme heat; stem rot can develop above 85°F (30°C). Spray or mist with water to clean. Apply high phosphate fertilizer at half recommended strength every 3-6 weeks while growing, every 6-12 weeks when growth slows. Dry and cool air causes premature flower drop. Dry and wet soil cause root loss. Leach regularly to avoid salts damage to delicate shallow, fibrous roots. White and brown dead areas on leaves can indicate sun-scorch. Check for spider mites, scale insects, whitefly, and mealybugs.

C. **'Chocolate Soldier':** large-leaved hybrid with gleaming red-brown foliage on upright and trailing stems.
C. **'Early Bird':** pointed green leaves, yellow-orange flowers.
C. **'Great Horned':** wide open-mouthed blossoms in yellow-orange; deep red-green leaves.

C. erythrophaea (e-rith-roh-FAY-a)
Long, 2-2½" (5-6.5cm) dark green leaves on arching, trailing stems. Orange flowers.

C. gloriosa (gloh-ri-OH-sa)
Trailing stems clothed with pairs of velvety leaves. Orange-red flowers extend beyond leafy cover.

C. lepidocaula (le-pi-doh-KAW-la)
Goldfish Plant
Low-growing. Deep green foliage and yellow-orange flowers.

C. linearis (li-nee-AH-ris)
Goldfish Plant
Silky rose-pink flowers, slender blue-green foliage.

C. microphylla (my-kroh-FIL-a)
Small-leaved Goldfish Vine
Arched, trailing stems lined with leafy pairs of tiny, dark green leaves that are dwarfed by orange-red flowers.

C. pilosissima (py-loh-SIS-i-ma)
Dark orange-red flowers.

C. sanguinolenta (san-gwi-noh-LEN-ta)
Upright, arching stems bear 4" (10cm) green leaves. Scarlet flowers.

Cordyline terminalis

Crassula ovata 'Minima'

Crassula ovata

CORDYLINE (kor-di-LY-nee)   ML - WA - PD
C. terminalis cultivars (ter-mi-NAH-lis)
Good-luck Plant, Dracaena Palm, Hawaiian Ti
Small palm-like tree has irregularly striped leaves. Colorful foliage arches from main stem. Many named cultivars. Height 3-6' (0.9-1.8m). Tolerates as cool as 50°F (10°C) for short periods. Grow in general indoor mix. Propagate from stem cuttings or by division. Air layering or tip cutting renews top of over-tall, leggy plant; sections of cane yield easily-rooted stem cuttings; rooted stump will regenerate.
MAINTENANCE Water often to supply plants' needs during active growth; in fall and winter, let soil become drier between waterings. Prune back hard to renew leggy, overgrown plants. Fertilize every 1-2 months. Provide relative humidity 30% or more; brown leaf margins may indicate dry air. Fluorides in soil and/or water also cause leaflet margin damage. Leaf spots result from wet foliage. Check for mealybugs, scale insects, spider mites.
'Kiwi': bright creamy green striped foliage has red edges.
'Red Sister': rich plum and deep burgundy leaves.

CRASSULA (KRAS-ew-la)   BL/ML - WA - DS
Succulent leaves on thick, branching stems. Long lived and slow growing. Tolerate low light conditions, cool temperatures. Grow in well-draining sandy indoor mix; repot infrequently. Propagate from stem or leaf cuttings.
MAINTENANCE Let soil remain dry for longer periods between waterings in winter. Constantly moist soil or poor drainage causes yellow leaves and root loss. Clean leaves with moist cloth or gentle spray of water. Fertilize at half recommended strength every month in spring and summer; none in winter. Check for mealybugs.

C. arborescens (ar-boh-RES-enz)
Silver Jade Plant, Silver-dollar, Chinese Jade
Rounded gray-green leaves covered with fine red dots; red edges intensify in brighter light. Grows to 2-8' (0.6-2.4m).

C. ovata (oh-VAH-ta)
[*C. argentea* (ar-JEN-tee-a), *C. portulacea* (por-tew-LAY-see-a)]
Jade, Chinese Rubber Plant
Easily grown succulent, takes form of miniature tree. Branching stems. Leaf margins, undersides turn red in direct sun. Height 2-5' (0.6-1.5m).
'Minima' (MIN-ee-ma), **Miniature Jade Plant:** miniature leaves.
'Tricolor' (TRY-co-lor), **Tricolor Jade Plant:** crisp white and deeper green markings.
'Variegata' (ve-ri-e-GAH-ta), **Variegated Jade Plant:** Longitudinal leaf markings in green, blue-gray, and cream.

Crossandra infundibuliformis

Cryptanthus bivittatus 'Starlight'

Cryptanthus bivittatus 'Pink Starlight'

Cryptanthus lacerdae

CROSSANDRA (kro-SAN-dra) ML/BL - WA - H - MS
C. infundibuliformis cultivars (in-fun-di-bew-li-FOR-mis)
Firecracker Flower

Flowering foliage plant grows 12-18" (30-45cm) high. Glossy, dark green foliage. Short yet showy, long-lasting spikes of orange, salmon, or yellow blossoms appear in summer, continue all year in good light. Repot when rootbound, using well-draining humusy indoor mix.
AFTER FLOWERING, trim off dying parts. If growth slows, reduce water and fertilizer applications, and let soil surface become dry between waterings in winter. Resume applications as new growth develops.
MAINTENANCE Shade from direct sun in summer. Water with tepid water and discard excess. Clean with gentle spray of tepid water. Fertilize at half recommended strength every 2-4 weeks during growth and flowering. Leach regularly to avoid damaging accumulation of soluble salts. Leaf curl results from dry air. Roots will rot in poorly drained or cool, wet soil. Check for whitefly.

CRYPTANTHUS (krip-TAN-thus) ML - WA - PD
Earth Star

Flat, star-like rosettes of colorful foliage. Inconspicuous white flowers in summer. Tolerate low light, develop best color in bright indirect light. Repotting rarely needed. Grow in porous, slightly acid bromeliad mix with added leaf mold or topsoil. Propagate from slow-rooting offsets, removed when about one-quarter the size of parent plant. Reported effective in tests to freshen or purify air (page 4).
MAINTENANCE Clean as needed with gentle spray of warm water. Fertilize every 2-3 months, less often during winter. Provide relative humidity 30% or more. Weakness and rotting results from overwatering. Check for scale insects and mealybugs.

C. 'Feuerzauber' (few-er-ZOW-ber): colorful yet almost translucent plant with silvery cross-bands. Color intensifies in bright indirect light.

C. 'Mars': rich silvery stripes sparkle on purple-green leafy rosette. Tolerates low light.

C. acaulis (a-KAW-lis)
Starfish Plant, Green Earth Star
Narrow triangular sea-green leaves with undulating, serrated edges. Spreads 6-12" (15-30cm) across with height to about 4" (10cm).

C. bivittatus (by-vi-TAH-tus)
Dwarf Rose-stripe Star
Neat rosettes spread 5-10" (13-25cm), mound to 6" (15cm). Colorful leaves have creamy stripes that blush bronze-pink in bright light.

Cycas revoluta

Cyclamen persicum

Cyclamen persicum

Cyclamen persicum

'Pink Starlight': predominantly pink leaves have dark and light green striped midribs. Small rosettes rarely exceed 6" (15cm).
'Ruby': entire plant ruby red with black stripes.
'Starlight': green-edged pink leaves. Best color in bright diffused light.

C. fosterianus (fos-te-ree-AH-nus)
Red-bronzed leaves with distinct silvery buff striping.

C. lacerdae (la SER-dee)
Silver Star
Miniature star has green and silver striped leaves. Rarely exceeds 4" (10cm) across.

CYCAS (SY-kas)   ML - CA
Bread Palm, Conehead, Funeral Palm, Sago Cycas
Fern-like or palm-like trees. Thickened short trunks topped by symmetrical arching clusters of big, stiff, dark green split leaves. Male and larger female cones on separate plants. Slow growth. Tolerates lower temperatures. Avoid hot, dry, unmoving air. Repot as needed in well-draining general indoor mix with some added humus.
MAINTENANCE Avoid splashing water onto fuzzy terminal bud area at base of leaves. In winter, let soil dry more between waterings. Fertilize every 2-3 months spring through fall. Trim damaged and discolored foliage. Check for scale insects.

C. circinalis (sir-sin-AH-lis)   **MS**
Sago Palm, Fern Palm, Queen Sago
Larger species resembles tropical palm. Leaflets have flattened edges. Heavy trunk can reach 10-15' (3-4.5m) and more, with leaves 4-6' (1.2-1.8m) long. Keep rich, humusy palm mix lightly moist.

C. revoluta (re-vo-LOO-ta)   **PD**
Sago Palm, King Sago, Japanese Sago Palm, Japanese Fern Palm
Dark green leaflets have rolled edges. Height and spread 2-8' (0.6-2.4m). Handsome leafy rosette best viewed from above or side: display on low table or floor, indoors, patio, larger plantings. Place where stiff leaves are away from traffic area.

CYCLAMEN (SIK-la-men)   BL/ML - CA - PD
***C. persicum* cultivars** (PER-si-kum)
Florist's Cyclamen
Seasonal flowering plant often has highly ornamental foliage. Colorful, waxy blossoms rise above leafy mass in winter or spring, last several weeks in draft-free location. Plant corm-like tuber, with smooth convex side down and crown above soil level, in humusy indoor mix. Propagate by division of healthy tubers. Many named cultivars and strains in different sizes.
'Giganteum' (jy-GAN-tee-um): familiar cyclamen with cluster of large

55

Cyrtomium falcatum

Davallia fejeensis

Cyrtomium falcatum 'Rochfordianum'

Davallia trichomanoides

Cyclamen (cont.)

flowers 10-15" (25-38cm) high. Foliage spreads 8-12" (20-30cm).
AFTER FLOWERING, continue to water and fertilize regularly while
new leaves develop. As leaves die down, reduce watering frequency
and stop fertilizing. Once all top growth has died, let soil dry for short
time. Remove dead leaves and replant in fresh soil. Water well. Place
in bright indirect light. When new leaves develop, resume fertilizing.
MAINTENANCE Best in bright indirect light, nights at 50-55°F (10-
13°C) and days at about 68°F (20°C). Let soil dry almost completely
between waterings. Fertilize at half recommended strength every 2
weeks while flowering; at full strength every 2-4 weeks while growing
without flowers. Reduce to half strength once flowers appear. Best
with relative humidity 30% or more. Trim out yellowed leaves and
dying flower stems. Keep leaves and crown dry to avoid rots. Check
for cyclamen mites, mealybugs.

CYRTOMIUM (sur-TOH-mi-um) ML/LL - CA - PD
C. falcatum (fal-KAH-tum)
Holly Fern, Japanese Holly Fern, Fishtail Fern

Durable and easily grown half-hardy fern with glossy, leathery foliage.
Big holly-like leaflets emerge from tightly rolled fronds. Height 12-
24" (30-60cm), spread 12-18" (30-45cm) or more. Specimen for table

or basket; leafy contrast in group planting, interiorscape. Grow outdoors in warm-temperate climates. Tolerates dry soil for short periods. Slow growing. Scaly rhizomes. Plant, with rhizome at or above
soil surface, in basic fern mix. Propagate by division. Several named
cultivars.

'Butterfieldii', Japanese Holly Fern: compact habit.
'Rochfordianum': broad, finely toothed leaflets.
MAINTENANCE Best in cooler, airy indoor climates. In winter, let soil
dry more between waterings; over-wet soil can result in crown rot.
Benefits from moderate sunlight during colder weather. Spray with
tepid water to remove dust. Fertilize at one-quarter recommended
strength every 4-6 weeks while new fronds are developing. Best with
relative humidity 30% or more; tolerates drier air than many ferns.
To renew plant, cut back to soil level. Mulch outdoors to protect roots
from frost. Check for scale insects, and for slugs and snails around
ferns from outdoors. Sensitive to chemical sprays.

DAVALLIA (da-VAH-li-a) ML/BL - WA - H - PD
Hare's-foot Fern

Small epiphytic ferns for warm, airy, humid locations. Woolly rhizomes extend from container. Triangular fronds resemble carrot foliage.
Grow on osmunda ball or in wire basket so rhizomes are exposed to
air; or place rhizomes on soil surface. Fibrous roots grow from rhi-

Dendrobium superbum

Dendrobium delicatum

Dendrobium 'Kingrose'

Dendrobium cobbianum

Dendrobium amethystoglossum

Dendrobium nobile 'Virginale'

zomes that touch soil; pin or peg rhizomes in place to encourage root-ing. Grow on osmunda fibers, tree fern pot, or in humus-rich fern mix. Propagate by division.

MAINTENANCE Adapts to light levels from bright indirect to partial shade; avoid direct scorching sun. Spray with tepid water to remove dust. Fertilize at one-quarter recommended strength every 4-6 weeks, or with weaker solution at every watering while growth is active. Delicate roots can be damaged by stronger applications. As growth slows, reduce watering and fertilizing frequency. Cut off old and dis-colored fronds. Sensitive to chemical sprays.

D. fejeensis (fee-jee-EN-sis)
Rabbit's Foot Fern
Fronds grow to about 18" (45cm) long, arching and trailing.
'Plumosa' (ploo-MOH-sa): feathery, graceful fronds.

D. trichomanoides (tri-koh-mah-NOI-deez)
Squirrel's Foot Fern
Delicate, finely divided, fronds grow about 6" (15cm) long.

DENDROBIUM (den-DROH-bi-um) ML/BL - WA - H - DS
Tropical and warm-climate orchids. Spring flowers in smooth, glow-ing colors, 1½-3" (4-8cm) across, borne in variable clusters. Plants may have long, pendulous stems or clustering short ones, with ever-green or deciduous leaves. Grow with shade outdoors in summer. Epiphytic: mount to hang in humid greenhouse climate. For indoor containers use well-draining, moisture retaining mix containing both fibrous and water-holding materials: osmunda, coarsely shredded fir bark, redwood chips, or small pumice stones, with coarse peat moss and/or perlite. Or use ready-made epiphytic orchid mix. Reduce depth of growing medium with deep underlayer of clean broken pot. Fleshy roots have pale outer layer. Repot in spring every few years to renew soil. Propagate by division into smaller clusters of swollen stems (pseu-dobulbs), from cuttings of longer stemmed varieties, or from plantlets growing at nodes.

AFTER FLOWERING, maintain regular watering and fertilizing while plant continues to grow. Reduce frequency as growth slows in fall and winter. Let soil of deciduous varieties dry more than that of evergreen plants. Cooler climate, drier soil, and brighter light stimulate *Dendrodium* flowering.

MAINTENANCE Avoid direct scorching sun in summer. While grow-ing, water thoroughly as soon as soil is dry. Fertilize every 2-4 weeks while growing. Root rot results from poor drainage, overwatering. Dark leaves and soft new growth result from insufficient light. Check for slugs and snails on outdoor orchids, and for spider mites, scale insects, mealybugs, rots, and leafspot on those indoors.

Dieffenbachia 'Paradise'

Dieffenbachia 'Tropic Snow'

Dieffenbachia 'Tropic Alix'

Dieffenbachia maculata 'Camille'

DIEFFENBACHIA (dee-fen-BAH-ki-a)   **ML - WA - PD/DS**
Dumb Cane, Mother-in-law's Tongue Plant, Tuftroot

Showy foliage plants have many named cultivars with variations of white, creamy-white, yellow, and green markings. Big leaves arch from upright cane growing as single stem or in cluster. Easily grown; tolerate shade, low light conditions, and occasional drought. Grow in well-draining humusy indoor mix; repot as needed to accommodate growing root ball. Propagate from stem cuttings or by division. Air layering or tip cutting renews top of over-tall, leggy plant; sections of cane yield stem cuttings; rooted stump will regenerate.

Reported effective in tests to freshen or purify air (page 4).

MAINTENANCE Best with night temperature above 60°F (16°C). During winter and in higher humidity environments, let soil dry out between waterings. Clean plants with gentle spray of tepid water. Fertilize at half recommended strength every 2-3 months. Trim off yellowed or damaged leaves to reduce chance of spreading disease. Overwatering encourages damage by leaf spot and rot organisms. Check for spider mites, mealybugs, scale insects, and thrips.

Note: Sap causes temporary swelling and irritation; avoid contact with mouth, eyes, and other sensitive skin areas.

D. **'Paradise':** bright white flecks over gray-green sheen on big, glossy leaves; dark green margins.

'Tropic Alix' ['Morloff']
and **'Tropic Snow'**
[*D. amoena* cultivars (a-MOI-na)]
Giant Dumb Cane
Biggest dieffenbachias with 15-20" (38-50cm) leaves on sturdy canes that grow to 6' (1.8m). 'Tropic Alix' has pale green and cream central variegations. 'Tropic Snow' foliage is densely creamy-yellow with dark green edges.

D. ×*bausei* (BOW-zee-y)
Broad, 12" (30cm) yellow-green leaves have irregular green patches and white spots.

D. maculata cultivars (ma-kew-LAH-ta)
[*D. picta* (PIK-ta)]
Spotted Dumb Cane
Leaves to 15" (38cm) long with irregular white markings.
'Camille': cream leaves have white veins, green edges.
'Exotica Compacta' (ek-ZOT-i-ka kom-PAK-ta): leaves marbled green and white. Compact habit.
'Rebecca': bright creamy white variegation.
'Snow Queen' ['Goldfinger', 'Lemon']: smooth pale lemon to creamy gold leaves have white midribs and veins, dark green edges.

Dionea muscipula

Dieffenbachia maculata 'Snow Queen'

Dieffenbachia maculata 'Exotica Compacta'

Dizygotheca elegantissima

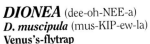

DIONEA (dee-oh-NEE-a)
D. muscipula (mus-KIP-ew-la)

BL - CA - H - MS

Venus's-flytrap

Insectivorous plant, native to the Carolinas. Novelty among indoor plants, forms low-growing cluster of yellow-green leaves 2-5" (5-13cm) long. Each leaf terminates with distinctive hinged trap that closes on intruding insects. Traps turn red in bright sun. White flowers form in spring. Develops tiny bulbs. Grow in half pots or terrarium, with very acid mix (pH 4.0-4.5) containing equal volumes of peat moss and washed sharp sand. Propagate by division or from seed.

MAINTENANCE Best in bright light and full sun. Provide shade when temperature exceeds 90°F (32°C). Best winter minimum temperature is 50°F (10°C). Water with distilled or soft rainwater to avoid damaging lime contamination. Maintain moist soil spring through fall by setting container in 1/2-1" (1.5-2.5cm) soft limefree or distilled water. Let soil become partly dry during slower growth or dormancy in winter. Carefully clip out old, discolored leaves. Do not fertilize, especially if Venus's-flytrap can be moved to semi-shaded outdoor area in warm weather. Traps do not develop correctly if plant is well-nourished; added chemicals may also damage sensitive plant tissues.

DIZYGOTHECA (di-zi-go-THEE-ka)
D. elegantissima (e-le-gan-TIS-i-ma)
[Schefflera elegantissima (shef-LEE-ra)]

ML/BL - WA - PD

False Aralia

Graceful slender tree grows indoors 4-8' (1.2-2.4m) or taller. Dainty, palmately divided leaves are coppery green; leaflets have toothed or wavy edges. Dark glossy stems pricked with creamy specks. Juvenile form of evergreen outdoor shrub for warm climates tolerates lower light as plant ages. Seedlings for terrarium or dish garden. Larger specimen or accent for low table, floor; lacy contrast in group planting, interiorscapes. Grow in general indoor mix. Propagate from cuttings.

MAINTENANCE Protect from direct, scorching summer sun. In winter, let soil become dry between waterings. Cut back straggly stems to stimulate fresh bushy growth. Clean with spray of tepid water. Fertilize every 1-2 months while growing, none during winter. Leaf drop results from soil that is too wet or too dry. Check for mealybugs, spider mites, scale insects.

WATERING (page 8)
MS - Keep soil moist.
PD - Let soil become partly dry between waterings.
DS - Allow soil to dry out between thorough waterings.

Dracaena deremensis 'Janet Craig'

Dracaena marginata

Dracaena fragrans 'Massangeana'

Dracaena reflexa

DRACAENA (dra-SEE-na)   **LL/ML/HL - WA - MS**

Tropical foliage with many variations. Cane types will grow in plain water. Tolerate as cool as 50°F (10°C) for short periods. Grow in general indoor mix. Propagate from stem cuttings or by division; air layering or tip cutting renews top of over-tall, leggy plants; sections of cane yield easily-rooted stem cuttings; rooted stumps regenerate.

D. deremensis, D. fragrans, and *D. marginata* reported effective in tests to freshen or purify air (page 4).

MAINTENANCE Water often during active growth; when growth slows in low light conditions (fall and winter), let soil become drier between waterings. Prune to renew leggy, overgrown shoots. Spray with tepid water or wipe to clean. Fertilize every 2-3 months. Leach regularly to avoid harmful buildup of soluble salts. Best with relative humidity 30% or more. Fluorides in soil and/or water cause dead tips, margins, dry areas. Excessive moisture results in soft leaf spots and rots. Check for mealybugs, spider mites, scale insects.

D. arborea (ar-BOH-ree-a)   **ML**
Tree Dracaena
Smooth, pale trunk topped by cluster of 2-3' (60-90cm) long leaves.

D. deremensis cultivars (de-re-MEN-sis)   **ML/LL**
Upright stems with broad leaves provide solid dark green or striped displays. Avoid direct scorching sun.

'Janet Craig': long-lasting variety grows 6-10' (1.8-3.0m) tall and 3-4' (0.9-1.2m) wide. Needs space.

'Janet Craig Compacta': compact, with close-spaced, smaller leaves.

'Warneckei' (war-NEK-ee-y), **Striped Dracaena**, and **'Warneckei Jumbo':** distinctive white stripes on dark green leaves.

D. draco (DRAY-koh)   **ML/BL**
Dragon Tree, Dragontree
Large dracaena with cluster of 24" (60cm) gray-green leaves on thick stem. Leaf edges turn red in sunlight. Height 2-6' (0.6-1.8m) indoors.

D. fragrans cultivars (FRAH-granz)   **ML/LL**
Corn Plant
Broad, arching leaves on corn-like plants; height to about 6' (1.8m). Easy to grow.

'Massangeana' (ma-san-jee-AH-na), **Corn(stalk) Plant, Massange's Dracaena:** clusters of yellow-banded leaves.

D. marginata (mar-ji-NAH-ta)   **ML**
Red-margined Dracaena, Madagascar Dragon Tree
Robust, easily grown plant. Slender stems and narrow 24" (60cm) dark green leaves with red margins. Fluorides cause minor leaf tip injury.

'Tricolor': green, gold, and red striped foliage needs brighter light.

Dyckia brevifolia

Dracaena marginata 'Tri-color'

Dyckia fosteriana

D. reflexa (ree-FLEK-sa)   **PD**
[*Pleomele reflexa* (PLEE-oh-meel)]
Song of India
Dark green or variegated reflexed leaves on flexible stems. Durable. Let soil dry between waterings. Several named cultivars.

D. sanderiana (san-de-ree-AH-na)   **ML**
Sander's Dracaena, Ribbon Plant
Graceful yet tough fountain of 9" (23cm) green and white striped leaves. Small plants for dish gardens.

D. surculosa (sur-kew-LOH-sa)
[*D. godseffiana* (god-se-fee-AH-na)]
Gold-dust Dracaena
Shrubby plant with slender, wiry stems. Cream-gold speckles on dark green leaves.
'Florida Beauty': heavier white spotting.
Additional cultivar: **'Juanita'.**

D. thalioides (tha-lee-OI-deez)
[*Pleomele thalioides*]
Lance Dracaena
Glossy, dark green leaves rise and spread in clusters.

DYCKIA (DY-ki-a, DIK-i-a)   **BL - WA - DS**
Robust terrestrial bromeliads well adapted to hot, dry conditions. Stiff, spiny leaves. Small flowers in spikes rising from leafy rosettes. Tolerate neglect and long periods of full sun. Small root systems. Grow in coarse bromeliad mix or sandy indoor mix. Repot rarely. Propagate from offsets or by division in spring.
AFTER FLOWERING, divide rosettes and repot if needed.
MAINTENANCE Soil can remain dry for long periods in winter. Clean leafy rosettes with brush or gentle stream of water. Fertilize every 1-2 months in spring and summer, every 2-3 months in fall and winter. Trim damaged, discolored parts.

D. brevifolia (bre-vi-FOH-li-a)
Pineapple Dyckia
Shiny green leaves with toothed edges, silvery undersides. Rosette can grow to 18" (45cm) high and 6-12" (15-30cm) across. Dense cluster of rosettes can spread to 20" (50cm). Orange flowers.

D. fosteriana (fos-te-ree-AH-na)
Small rosettes, to 4" (10cm) high and 6-12" (15-30cm) across. Narrow, toothed, gray leaves take on bronze tone in full sun. Flowers golden yellow. Forms large, attractive cluster.

Echinocactus grusonii

Epidendrum lancifolium

Epidendrum dichromum

Epidendrum odoratissimum

ECHINOCACTUS (e-kee-noh-KAK-tus) **BL - WA - CA - DS**
E. grusonii (groo-SOH-nee-y)
Barrel Cactus, Golden Barrel, Golden-ball
Symmetrical cactus has single or clustered rounded light green stems with strong golden spines. Older plant growing in sunlight produces yellow flowers in spring. Tolerates lower light. Grows slowly to 3-4' (0.9-1.2m) high and 2½' (75cm) across. Plant in sandy indoor mix.
MAINTENANCE Provide warm temperatures when growing and cool when dormant, usually in winter. Water sparingly during dormancy. Fertilize at half recommended strength every month in spring and summer. Rotting can result from overwatering and excess humidity.

EPIDENDRUM (e-pi-DEN-drum) **ML - CA/WA - H - DS**
Buttonhole Orchid
Tropical and cooler-climate orchids are among easiest for indoors. Flowers freely, with sparkling clusters of small colorful blossoms. Plants have long, pendulous stems or short clustering ones. Grow with shade outdoors. Epiphytic: mount to hang in humid greenhouse. Plant in well-draining, moisture retaining mix containing both fibrous and water-holding materials, or use ready-made epiphytic orchid mix. Reduce depth of mix with deep underlayer of clean broken pot. Repot

in spring every few years. Propagate by division of swollen stems (pseudobulbs) or from cuttings of longer stems.
AFTER FLOWERING, maintain regular watering and fertilizing while plant continues to grow. Reduce frequency as growth slows. Let soil of clustering varieties (with pseudobulbs) dry more than that of taller, long-stemmed plants.
MAINTENANCE Avoid direct scorching sun in summer. Best with minimum night temperatures of 50-55°F (10-13°C), and days at about 70°F (21°C). While growing, water thoroughly as soon as soil is dry. Fertilize every 2-4 weeks while growing. Root rot results from poor drainage, overwatering. Dark leaves and soft new growth result from insufficient light. Check for slugs and snails on outdoor orchids; and indoors for spider mites, scale insects, mealybugs, rots, and leafspot.

EPIPREMNUM (e-pi-PREM-num) **ML - WA - PD/DS**
E. aureum and cultivars (AW-ree-um)
[*Scindapsus aureus* (skin-DAP-sus AW-ree-us)]
Pothos, Golden Pothos, Devil's Ivy, Taro Vine
Tropical foliage vine has crisp, shiny leaves on slender trailing and climbing stems. Gold markings on 2-4" (5-10cm) leaves. Good basket plant; also grows well in plain water. Easy to grow; fleshy roots withstand occasional drought. Grow in general indoor mix; repot infre-

Epipremnum aureum 'Marble Queen'

Episcia cupreata 'Chocolate Soldier'

Epipremnum aureum 'Mayan Gold'

Episcia dianthiflora

quently. Propagate from stem cuttings.

Reported effective in tests to freshen or purify air (page 4).

'Marble Queen', Silver Pothos: smooth, waxy leaves variegated with white, especially when young.

'Mayan Gold': golden yellow variegations.

Additional cultivar: **'Jade'** ['Tropic Green'].

MAINTENANCE Prefers shade with no direct sunlight. Allow soil to dry more between waterings when growth is slower in winter. Leaf size increases as plants mature: trim long, straggly stems to encourage new juvenile growth. Remove faded or yellowing leaves. Fertilize every 3 months, or apply at half recommended strength every 4-6 weeks. Leach regularly to avoid damaging accumulation of soluable salts. Excess water can result in root rots. Check for scale insects.

EPISCIA (e-PIS-i-a)   ML/BL - WA - H - PD

Spreading, tropical gesneriads with distinctive flowers, many with colorful quilted foliage. Flowers constantly in brightly lighted conditions. Leafy rosettes form on stolons or runners. Good basket plant. Shallow, fibrous roots. Grow in basic gesneriad mix. Repot infrequently. Propagate by division, from plantlets, leaf cuttings. Many named cultivars.

AFTER FLOWERING, maintain growth with regular watering and feeding, reducing to match slower growth in low light and tempera-

ture conditions. Trim off stolons (runners) to encourage reflowering.

MAINTENANCE Shade from strong sun in summer and outdoors. Best with bright indirect light, at 60°F (16°C) or more, and high humidity. Apply high phosphate fertilizer at half strength every 4-6 weeks while growing vigorously. Fully dry or constantly wet soil causes root loss. Leach regularly to avoid salts damage to delicate roots. Leaves lost as plants become dormant in cooler air. White and brown dead areas on leaves can indicate sun-scorch. Check for root rots, spider mites, and mealybugs.

E. **'Cygnet':** frilly white flowers; green leaves.

E. **'La Solidad':** distinctive markings on broad, dark green leaves.

E. **'Moss Agate':** corrugated, puckered foliage; crimson flowers.

E. **'Pink Brocade':** vivid pink edge on silvered leaves; orange-red blooms.

E. cupreata cultivars (kew-pree-AH-ta)

'Chocolate Soldier': quilted chocolate-colored leaves mound 4-6" (10-15cm). Flowers red.

'Silver Sheen': striking silvery markings; red flowers.

E. dianthiflora (dee-an-thi-FLOH-ra)

[*Alsobia dianthiflora* (al-SOH-bi-a)]

Lace Flower Vine

Small rosettes of green leaves and fringed white flowers.

Espostoa lanata

Euphorbia trigona

Euphorbia milii var. *splendens*

ESPOSTOA (es-pos-TOH-a)   BL - WA/CA - DS
E. lanata (la-NAH-ta)
Cottonball, Snowball Cactus, Peruvian Old-man
Columnar branching cactus has green stem covered with long soft white hairs that cover the sharp spines. Grows to 1-2' (60-90cm) indoors, without blossom. Flowers when about 30 years old. Specimen or accent. Tolerates some shade. Very slow growing. Fibrous roots. Grow in sandy indoor mix. Propagate from seed.
MAINTENANCE Provide warm temperatures when growing and cool when dormant, usually in winter. Water sparingly during dormancy. Fertilize at half recommended strength every 2 months in spring and summer. Rotting can result from overwatering and excess humidity.

EUPHORBIA (ew-FOR-bi-a)   ML/BL - WA - PD/DS
Variable group of plants represented indoors by cactus-like succulents and colorful poinsettias. Tiny flowers nestle among colorful bracts. All are striking specimens or accents, useful in group plantings. Fibrous roots. Grow in sandy or well-draining general indoor mix; repot infrequently. Propagate from stem cuttings.
MAINTENANCE Let soil remain dry for longer periods between waterings in winter. Constantly moist soil or poor drainage causes stem

rots, yellowed, dropping leaves, and root losses. Clean succulent euphorbias with gentle spray of water. Fertilize succulents at half recommended strength every month spring through fall; none in winter. Fertilize poinsettias every month while flowering and growing. Provide relative humidity of 30% or more. Leaf drop may result from low humidity. Check for whitefly, mealybugs, and scale.

Note: Milky sap of succulent euphorbias may cause severe dermatitis. However, poinsettia sap is not allergenic.

E. lactea (LAK-tee-a)
Candelabra Cactus, Hatrack Cactus, Dragon-bones
Spiny succulent with strong, curving branches. No flowers. Height to about 36" (90cm).
'Cristata' (kris-TAH-ta), **Crested Euphorbia, Frilled-fan, Elkhorn:** Broad stems are ruffled and crested.

E. milii var. splendens (MIL-ee-y SPLEN-denz)
[*E. splendens*]
Crown-of-thorns, Christ Thorn
Succulent, spiny plants with close-set leaves and small, brilliantly colored flower bracts. Sturdy branches grow 10-18" (25-45cm) long on 12-36" (30-90cm) plants. Flowers at any time, especially in winter and spring. Needs adequate light for flowering and leaf maintenance.

Euphorbia pulcherrima

Euphorbia pulcherrima

Euphorbia pulcherrima

Exacum affine

E. pulcherrima (pul-KE-ri-ma)   BL
Poinsettia, Christmas Star, Flor de Noche Buena

Seasonal flowering plant. Many named hybrids with longlasting bracts in white, cream, pink, red, and multicolored. Tolerates dry soil between thorough waterings. Pot and basket plant. Fertilize every month; inadequate fertilization may result in leaf drop.

Reported effective in tests to freshen or purify air (page 4).

AFTER FLOWERING, continue to water and fertilize regularly. Keep in brightly lighted location to stop lower leaves yellowing and dropping. In early spring, repot and trim to encourage strong new growth. If possible, grow outdoors during summer, in full sun (partial shade in the south). Or continue to maintain indoors in full sun. Move back indoors in fall when temperatures are likely to drop below 55°F (13°C). Flowers develop in response to longer nights of fall. Provide more than 12 hours of uninterrupted complete darkness each night from early October to December for holiday flowers. When bracts begin to develop color, return plants to normal indoor light conditions.

E. trigona (tri-GOH-na)
African Milk Tree, Abyssinian Euphorbia

Strongly vertical stems have spiny ridges and small leaves on upper, younger portions. No flowers.

EXACUM (EK-sa-kum)   ML/BL - WA - PD
E. affine (a-FEE-nee)
German Violet, Persian Violet, Arabian Gentian

Tender seasonal flowering plant. Blue-violet, lavender, or white blossoms open over several months. Leaves and stems are crisp, bright green. Height 12-24" (30-60cm). Specimen, decorator item for any position with sufficient light to maintain leaf color. Prefers warm, somewhat humid locations. Grown from seed sown in late summer and fall for spring flowers, in winter for summer display. Plant in well-draining, humusy indoor mix.

AFTER FLOWERING, plant dies back completely. Growth can be prolonged in greenhouse conditions.

MAINTENANCE Water thoroughly when soil surface is dry; avoid both completely dry and soggy soil conditions. Fertilize actively growing plant at half recommended strength every 2-4 weeks. Remove faded flowers and damaged or dying leaves. Best with relative humidity 30% or more. Check for whitefly.

Hanging plants use more water than others in the same room, so need more frequent waterings. Groups of plants in baskets, planters, dish gardens, etc. will grow together for the longest time if all have the same watering needs.

Fatsia japonica

Ferocactus acanthodes

Ficus benjamina

FATSIA (FAT-see-a) **ML/BL - CA - PD**
F. japonica (ja-PON-i-ka)
Japanese Aralia, Formosa Rice Tree, Paper Plant
Foliage shrub or tree with big, deeply lobed, maple-like leaves. Thick, flexible stems. Gleaming green leaves sometimes variegated white. Height 3-8' (0.9-2.4m). Easy to grow. Plant in general indoor mix; repot infrequently. Propagate from stem or root cuttings.
MAINTENANCE Avoid direct scorching sun. When growth is rapid, water when just soil surface is dry; in winter, let soil dry more between waterings. Fertilize at half recommended strength every 6-8 weeks in spring and summer only. Leach regularly to avoid damaging accumulation of soluble salts. Poor light, dry soil result in leaf drop. Wet conditions encourage rots. Check for aphids, spider mites, mealybugs, scale insects, and thrips.

FEROCACTUS (fe-roh-KAK-tus) **BL - WA/CA - DS**
Barrel Cactus, Fishhook Cactus, Visnaga
F. acanthodes (a-kan-THOH-deez)
[*F. cylindraceus* (si-lin-DRAY-see-us)]
Fire Barrel
Rounded barrel cactus has long, brilliant red, hooked spines. Can grow

3-4' (0.6-1.2m) across and high in container, to about 10' (3.0m) when planted outside. Summer flowers orange-red on plants 10" (25cm) and larger. Slow growing. Fibrous roots. Plant in sandy indoor mix.
MAINTENANCE Provide warm temperatures when growing and cool when dormant, usually in winter. Water sparingly during dormancy. Fertilize at half recommended strength every 2 months in spring and summer. Rotting can result from overwatering and excess humidity.

FICUS (FEE-kus, FY-kus) **ML - WA - PD/DS**
Fig
Tropical trees, shrubs, and woody vines long used for foliage plants indoors. Leaf sizes vary. Flowers insignificant, fruit small. Uses vary, from large specimen trees to hanging baskets. Good for interiorscapes. Fibrous roots. Plant in general indoor mix; repot infrequently. Propagate by stem cuttings, air-layering, and division of rooting creepers.
MAINTENANCE Tolerate temperatures as low as 50°F (10°C) for short periods. Let soil dry more between waterings in winter when growth is slow. Fertilize at half recommended strength every 6-8 weeks spring through fall. Cold drafts, prolonged dry soil, and sudden climate changes result in leaf losses. Check for spider mites, scale insects, mealy bugs, and whitefly.

Ficus pumila 'Curly'

Ficus lyrata

Ficus elastica 'Decora'

Ficus pumila

F. benjamina and cultivars (ben-ja-MEE-na)
[*F. retusa* var. *nitida* (re-TEW-sa NIT-i-da)]
Weeping Fig
Small-leaved, branching trees grow slowly to 6-18' (1.8-5.4m). Leaves often drop in new location; new ones grow on bare branches. Foliage solid green or variegated white or cream. Prune to shape after main flush of growth to minimize loss of white latex sap. Easy to grow.
'Citation': curled leaves.
'Stacey': larger, darker green leaves spaced more closely, more tolerant than species.
Additional cultivars: **'Jacqueline', 'Wintergreen', 'Spearmint'.**

F. elastica cultivars (e-LAS-ti-ka)
India Rubber Plant
Single-stem tree with big, gleaming, oval leaves. Several stems grow together for fuller specimen. Drafts cause leaf drop. Easy to grow.
'Decora' (de-KOH-ra), **Wideleaf Rubber Plant:** leaves bronze-red when young; red stem and lower midrib.
'Robusta' (roh-BUS-ta): tolerates and adapts to low light conditions.
'Rubra' (ROO-bra): reddish young leaves mature with red edges.
'Honduras', Variegated Rubber Plant: creamy or gray-green striping and segmenting on broad, leathery leaves.

F. lyrata and cultivars (ly-RAH-ta)
[*F. pandurata* (pan-dew-RAH-ta)]
Fiddleleaf Fig
Huge, dramatic, shapely leaves on erect and branching tree for spacious location. Height 5' (1.5m) and more.
'Compacta' (kom-PAK-ta): smaller leaves, more compact habit.

F. pumila (PEW-mi-la)
[*F. repens* (REE-penz)]
Creeping Fig
Creeping, trailing stems root where they touch soil. Free-branching variety likes fresh air but not drafts. Good basket plant.
'Curly', Flame Leaf Creeping Fig: vigorous open creeper has lobed, quilted foliage leaves, with pale green (flash) in centers.

F. retusa cultivars (re-TEW-sa)
[*F. microcarpa* (mik-roh-KAR-pa)]
Indian Laurel
Similar to Weeping Fig with broader, bigger leaves and more upright habit. Useful large specimen. Several named cultivars.

Fittonia verschaffeltii var. argyroneura

Fittonia verschaffeltii var. pearcei

Fittonia verschaffeltii var. argyroneura 'Nana'

Foeniculum vulgare: fennel

FITTONIA (fi-TON-i-a)   LL/ML - WA - PD
F. verschaffeltii varieties (ver-sha-FEL-tee-y)
Mosaic Plant, Nerve Plant, Red-nerve Plant

Low-growing ornamental foliage plants for shady, somewhat humid places. Branching stems spread horizontally to 12-18"(30-45cm). Dark olive leaves have contrasting red veins. Mounds 4-6" (10-15cm). Ground cover, specimen or accent, hanging basket, dish garden, terrarium plants. Shallow, fibrous roots. Plant in well-draining indoor mix; repot infrequently before spring flush of growth. Propagate from stem cuttings, by division.

F. v. var. argyroneura (ar-gy-ro-NEW-ra)
Silver-nerve Plant
Delicate silver-white veins contrast vivid green leaf color.
'Nana' ['Minima']: small-scale silver-nerve plant, ideal for terrariums, smaller plant grouping.

F. v. var. pearcei (PEER-see-eye)
Pink Nerve Plant
Slightly quilted leaves have carmine pink veins and midrib.

MAINTENANCE Avoid direct scorching sun. Let soil dry more between waterings during winter. Low light results in spindly growth. Trim to shape and remove damaged parts to reduce potential infection sites. Fertilize at half recommended strength every 2-3 months. Leach regularly to avoid salts damage to delicate roots. Best with relative humidity 30% or more. Needs air movement to prevent rotting. Check for whitefly, spider mites.

FOENICULUM (fee-NIK-ew-lum)   BL - CA - MS
F. vulgare varieties (vul-GAH-ree)
Fennel

Aromatic perennial herb best grown as annual. Grows rapidly. Looks like dill, but fine-cut foliage is bright green. Anise-flavored leaves used with seafood and in fish sauces; seeds flavor breads, pastries, sweet pickles. Start from seed or pot young plants in general indoor mix. MAINTENANCE Trim regularly to contain size. Fertilize at half recommended strength every 2-4 weeks when growth is vigorous; every 4-8 weeks during winter. Wash with water to discourage spider mites.

F. v. var. azoricum (a-ZOH-ri-kum), **Finnochio, Florence Fennel, Anise:** milder flavor, lower-growing, has thickened, edible leaf bases.

F. v. var. dulce (DUL-kay, DUL-chay), **Sweet Fennel:** most commonly grown fennel.

Fuchsia X *hybrida*

Gardenia jasminoides

FUCHSIA (FOOK-si-a, FEW-sha)   ML - CA - MS/PD
F. X *hybrida* (HYB-ri-da)
Lady's Eardrops

Shrubby flowering plants for cool, somewhat humid indoor areas, outdoors in temperate climates. Many named cultivars. Colorful, showy
blossoms in spring and summer. Slender, woody stems arch and droop;
some varieties naturally pendulous. Grow from seasonal bloom on
porch, patio, outdoors in more humid climates. Useful basket, container, bedding plants. Fibrous roots. Fuchisa grows rapidly after dormancy; repot in early spring, using well-draining general or humusy
indoor mix. Propagate from stem cuttings taken in late summer before
shoots harden.

AFTER FLOWERING, let soil dry more between waterings as leaves
die. Reduce fertilizer applications to match growth rate; none at all
during dormancy. As new growth begins in spring, increase frequency of water and fertilizer applications. Prune to shape as desired.
MAINTENANCE Avoid direct scorching sun. Keep soil moist while
growth is rapid and flowers are developing. Fertilize at half recommended rate every 2-3 weeks while growing and flowering. Best with
relative humidity 30% or more. Heat, wet or dry soil, and dry air cause
loss of flowers and leaves. Check for whitefly, spider mites.

GARDENIA (gar-DEN-i-a)   ML/BL - WA - H - MS/PD
G. jasminoides (jas-mi-NOI-deez)
[*G. augusta* (aw-GUS-ta)]
Gardenia, Cape Jasmine

Flowering evergreen shrub grows 12-36" (30-90cm) high. Deliciously
scented blossoms open from summer, all year in areas with sufficient
light. Specimen or accent in flower, otherwise fine glossy-leaved evergreen for plant groups. Tolerates temperatures cooler than 60°F (16°C)
for short periods. Fibrous roots. Grow in well-draining, neutral to acid,
humusy indoor mix; repot infrequently. Propagate in spring or summer from stem cuttings.

MAINTENANCE Protect from direct summer sun. Keep soil moist
but not soggy while flowers develop; let soil dry more when growth is
slower or air is cooler. Best flower development with 60-65°F (16-18°C)
nights, bright diffused light, and high humidity. Prune to shape. Apply
acid fertilizer every 4-6 weeks spring and summer. Leach regularly to
avoid damaging accumulation of soluble salts. Flower bud drop can
result from drafts, soil too wet or too dry, and low light conditions.
Check for whitefly, mealybugs, spider mites, scale insects.

Gasteria

Gerbera jamesonii

Gibasis pellucida

GASTERIA (gas-TEH-ri-a)　　　ML - WA - DS
Ox Tongue, Pencil-leaf

Small succulent members of the lily family with clustered leathery, strap-like leaves. Foliage dark green mottled, bronzed, sometimes warty. Long-stemmed flower clusters may develop in summer. Tolerate lower light than other succulents. Grow in sandy indoor mix; repot infrequently. Propagate by division, or from leaf cuttings or seed.
MAINTENANCE   Let soil remain dry for longer periods between waterings in winter. Constantly moist soil or poor drainage causes yellow leaves and root loss. Fertilize at half recommended strength every month in spring and summer; none in winter.

GERBERA (GER-be-ra)　　　BL - WA - PD
G. jamesonii hybrids (jaym-SON-ee-y)
Transvaal Daisy, Barberton Daisy

Flowering perennial for indoor use while in flower. Big, colorful daisy blossoms rise about 18" (45cm) above dense rosette of 8-12" (20-30cm) leaves. Many shades of red, orange, yellow, cream. Decorative accents to use singly or in groups. Plant outdoors in hot, drier areas; will not tolerate frost. Grow in sandy indoor mix. Grown from seed; can be propagated by division of clump and rhizome. Fertilize every 4-6 weeks while growing and flowering. Check for spider mites.
Reported effective in tests to freshen or purify air (page 4).

GIBASIS (gi-BAY-sis)　　　ML/BL - WA - PD
G. pellucida (pe-lew-SEE-da)
[*G. geniculata* (ge-ni-kew-LAH-ta)]
Tahitian Bridal Veil

Vigorous creeping and trailing plant, grows easily in warm, somewhat humid climates. Freely branching, dense growth with slender flexible stems and fresh green leaves, undersides purple. Clouds of tiny white blossoms give this plant its name. Flowers almost continuously once established and with good light. Useful basket plant. Grow in general indoor mix. Propagate by division or from stem cuttings.
MAINTENANCE   Shade from direct scorching sun. Dry air or soil cause wilting. Fertilize at half recommended strength every 4-8 weeks. Leach regularly to avoid salts damage to sensitive roots. Trim out straggly stems and pinch shoots regularly to encourage bushiness and fresh new growth. Check for aphids and spider mites.

Guzmania lingulata

Guzmania musaica

Guzmania lingulata var. *cardinalis*

Guzmania sanguinea

Guzmania lingulata var. *minor*

Guzmania lingulata 'Symfonie'

GUZMANIA (gooz-MAH-ni-a) ML/LL - WA - MS

Bromeliad with glossy rosettes of arched, spreading leaves and long-lasting flower clusters. Colorful accents for warm, low light positions. Small, fleshy root system; established plants rarely need repotting. Grow in porous, slightly acid bromeliad mix. Propagate in spring and summer from offsets and by division.

Reported effective in tests to freshen or purify air (page 4).

AFTER FLOWERING, remove dead flower stems. Young plants, or offsets, grow at plant base. When offsets are half the size of the parent plant, cut at base and pot separately.

MAINTENANCE Keep water in central cup at all times. Clean upper leaf surfaces gently with moist soft cloth. Fertilize at one-quarter recommended strength, applied to soil and cup every 4 weeks. Provide relative humidity 30% or more; brown leaf tips indicate dry air. Trim damaged, discolored parts. Mulch with fir bark to support newly potted or top-heavy plants. Check for scale insects, mealybugs, basal rot.

G. lingulata, cultivars and varieties (lin-gew-LAH-ta)
Height about 12" (30cm), spread 2-3' (60-90cm). Long-lasting flower clusters with white, pink, or red blossoms and variously colored bracts. Tolerate low light.

'Amaranth': scarlet bracts spread from upright flower cluster. Height 20-26" (50-65cm).

'Carine': bright red spreading bracts rest at center of green, leafy rosette. Height about 12" (30cm).

'Cherry': slender flower cluster with cherry-red bracts. Height 20-30" (50-75cm). Foliage green.

'Orangeade': clear orange bracts surround golden yellow flowers. Height 20-26" (50-65cm).

'Symfonie': large plant with gleaming green leaves that spread 2-4' (0.6-1.2m). Strong red coloring at plant center. Cluster of yellow flowers has red bracts and stem. Grows well in moderate light.

G. l. var. *cardinalis* (kar-di-NAH-lis), **Scarlet Star:** large, scarlet flower bracts.

G. l. var. *minor* (MY-nor), **Orange Star:** showy orange-red bracts surrounding white-yellow flowers.

'Vella': bright red bracts.

G. musaica (moo-ZAH-i-ka)
Dark green leaves with yellow cross-bands, purple undersides spread 30-36" (75-90cm).

G. sanguinea (san-GWIN-ee-a)
Formal rosette of stiff green foliage turns first yellow, then red that spreads from the top as flowers develop deep in the cup.

Gynura aurantiaca 'Purple Passion'

Haworthia fasciata

Hatoria salicornioides

Haworthia limifolia

GYNURA (gy-NEW-ra)   BL - WA - PD
G. aurantiaca 'Purple Passion' (aw-ran-tee-AH-ka)
Purple Passion Plant
Velvet-leaved trailing foliage plant with purple coloring over dark green. Easy for shelf, table, basket; colorful accent in plant groups, dish gardens. Grows well in plain water. Grow in general indoor mix; repot as needed. Propagate from stem cuttings.
MAINTENANCE Purple coloring lost with insufficient light. Flowers malodorous: remove before buds open. Trim off damaged and straggly growth. Apply half-strength fertilizer every 4 weeks. Leach regularly to avoid damaging accumulation of soluble salts. Check for whitefly, aphids, mealybugs, and spider mites.

HATIORA (ha-tee-OR-a)   ML - WA - H - PD
H. salicornioides (sa-li-kor-nee-OI-deez)
Dancing-bones Cactus, Drunkard's-dream
Much-branched epiphytic cactus grows to height and spread of 12" (30cm), though branches can hang longer in more humid climate. Club-shaped joints about 1" (2.5cm) long. Small yellow flowers in spring. Unusual specimen, basket plant. Fibrous roots. Grow in humusy indoor mix; repot infrequently. Propagate from stem cuttings.

MAINTENANCE Let soil remain dry for longer periods between waterings in winter. Fertilize at half recommended strength every 1-2 months.

HAWORTHIA (ha-WOR-thi-a)   ML - WA - DS
Small succulent members of the lily family with smooth or ridged leafy rosettes. Long-stemmed flower clusters. Windowsill or table accents; group plantings. Tolerate lower light than other succulents. Slow growing. Fibrous roots. Grow in sandy indoor mix; repot infrequently. Propagate by division or from seed.
MAINTENANCE Let soil remain dry for longer periods between waterings in winter. Clean with gentle spray of water. Fertilize at half recommended strength twice a year, spring and summer; none in winter.

H. fasciata (fa-see-AH-ta)
Zebra Plant
Raised white stripes across pointed dark green leaves. Height 3-6" (8-15cm). Spreads freely. Easy to grow.

H. limifolia (lee-mi-FOH-li-a)
Fairy-washboard
Fleshy, ridged leaves curve outwards to form low rosette, 3-6" (7.5-15cm) wide.

Hedera helix

Hedera canariensis 'Variegata'

Hedera helix 'Gold Dust'

Hedera helix 'Cavendishii'

Hedera helix 'Maple leaf'

HEDERA (HED-e-ra)   BL/ML - CA - PD

Evergreen woody vines that thrive in cooler indoor climates. Many sizes and shapes of green or variegated foliage. Use as small or large specimens; in terrariums, dish gardens; as ground cover for larger plantings; in baskets; and to climb or trail. Will grow in plain water. Plant outdoors in temperate climates. Most tolerate lower light conditions and cool temperatures. Grow in well-draining general indoor mix; repot as needed. Propagate from stem cuttings, division.

MAINTENANCE Pinch tips to encourage branching. Best with relative humidity 30% or more. Spray with water to clean. Fertilize at half recommended strength every 4-6 weeks. When growth is slower, reduce watering and fertilizing frequency. Cool, over-moist conditions result in rots. Check for spider mites, scale insects, mealybugs, and aphids.

H. canariensis and cultivars (ka-ne-ree-EN-sis)
Canary Island Ivy, Algerian Ivy

Gleaming, rich green leaves. Prefers warmth, 30% relative humidity.

'Variegata' (ve-ri-e-GAH-ta): creamy-white leaf edges become tinged red-purple in cooler air.

H. helix cultivars (HEE-liks)
English Ivy

Tolerant evergreen vines with strong, flexible stems that root easily in soil or water, on brick or wood. Easy to grow. Many named cultivars. Reported effective in tests to freshen or purify air (page 4).

'Cavendishii', Variegated Ivy: fresh to dark green leaves have bright creamy-white edges.

'Glacier': small, pointed leaves variegated gray-green and edged in pink and white.

'Goldchild': broad, flat leaves have creamy yellow margins and two-tone green mottled centers; grows slowly.

'Gold Dust': leaves mottled creamy-white.

'Hahn's Selfbranching': typical ivy-leaf foliage on bushy, branching vine forms dense mat.

'Kolibri' (koh-LIB-ree): irregular ivory-white to silver variegations spread from centers of dark green leaves.

'Maple Leaf' ['Maple Queen']: three-lobed leaves on red stems, paler green veins.

'Needlepoint': slender pointed leaves in formal rows on upturned stems.

'Scutifolia', Heartleaf Ivy: small heart-shaped matte green leaves.

'Tiger Eye': bright yellow centers to pointed lobed leaves on branching vine.

Hemigraphis 'Exotica'

Hibiscus rosa-sinensis

HEMIGRAPHIS (he-mi-GRAF-is) LL/ML - WA - PD

H. alternata (al-ter-NAH-ta)
[*H. colorata* (ko-lo-RAH-ta)]
Red Ivy
and
***H.* 'Exotica'** (ek-SOT-i-ka)
Purple Waffle Plant

Fast-growing creepers with unusual metallic red coloring under dark green leaves; color varies with environment. 'Exotica' has crinkled, bronze-red foliage. Red, fleshy stems. Easily grown ground cover, basket. Plant in general indoor mix. Propagate from stem cuttings.

MAINTENANCE Pinch frequently and prune stems for compact, bushy development. Apply half strength fertilizer every 4-8 weeks. Leach regularly to avoid salts damage to sensitive roots. Best with relative humidity 30% or more. When growth is slower, reduce watering and fertilizing frequency. Check for scale insects and spider mites.

LIGHT for indoor plants (page 6)
LL - LOW LIGHT: performs well in low light conditions, or shade.
ML - MODERATE LIGHT: performs well in part shade or diffused light.
BL - BRIGHT LIGHT: performs well in full sun or bright indirect light.

HIBISCUS (hy-BIS-kus) ML/BL - CA - PD/MS

H. rosa-sinensis cultivars (ROH-za-si-NEN-sis)
Hibiscus, Chinese Hibiscus, Rose-of-China

Tropical flowering shrub with big, brilliantly colored seasonal or year-round blossoms. Foliage dark green. Height in containers 18-36" (45-90cm). Accent or specimen in flower; attractive foliage shrub in group plantings. Grow outdoors in summer. Fibrous roots. Grow in general indoor mix; repot as needed in early spring. Propagate from stem cuttings in spring and summer.

AFTER FLOWERING, prune to contain size, reduce watering frequency, and stop fertilizing while plant rests. As fresh new growth is seen, increase watering frequency and resume fertilizer applications. Hibiscus will flower year-round with sufficient light and consistent humidity.

MAINTENANCE Keep soil moist but not soggy during flowering. Trim or prune lightly to shape. Best with relative humidity 30% or more. Fertilize at half recommended strength every 2-4 weeks spring and summer, every 4-8 weeks in fall and winter as long as growth continues. Leach regularly to avoid damaging accumulation of soluble salts. Drafts and uneven soil moisture can result in bud loss. Check for spider mites, whitefly, mealybugs, and scale insects.

Hippeastrum

Howea forsterana

HIPPEASTRUM (hi-pe-AS-trum)   **BL - WA - PD**
Amaryllis, Dutch Amaryllis
Tropical bulb produces large trumpet flowers on 12-24" (30-60cm) stem. Heavy, strap-shaped leaves. Striking plant in flower, can be reflowered successfully after one or more dormant periods. Fleshy roots and large bulb. Grow in general indoor mix; repot when new leaves show after dormancy. Propagate from bulblets that form beside parent.
AFTER FLOWERING, remove faded blossoms and continue to water as needed and fertilize monthly while leaves remain green. Gradually reduce watering and stop fertilizing as leaves die down. Keep dormant bulbs dry through summer. Repot in late fall. Increase watering and resume fertilizer applications as leaves and flowers develop.

HOWEA (HOW-ee-a)   **ML - CA - PD**
Sentry Palm
H. forsterana (for-ste-RAH-na)
Forster Sentry Palm, Kentia Palm, Thatch-leaf Palm
Tolerant feather palm for small and large containers. Broad leaflets on upright, slow-growing stems. Useful specimen or in larger grouping. Shelter from drafts. Easily grown; Shade tolerant. Plant in deep pot with well-draining, rich, humusy palm mix. Propagate from seed.
MAINTENANCE Water less often in winter. Wipe leaves or wash with water to remove dust. If possible, move to shaded outdoor position during warm months. Fertilize every month spring through fall. Trim damaged and discolored foliage. Brown leaf-tips may result from soil too dry or too wet. Check for spider mites, scale insects, and leaf spot.

HUMIDITY (page 7)
 H - Best with relative humidity 50% or more.

TEMPERATURE (page 7)
 CA - COOL to AVERAGE TEMPERATURES: days 60-75°F (16-24°C), nights as cool as 45°F (7°C).
 WA - AVERAGE to WARM TEMPERATURES: days 70-80°F (21-27°C), nights 60-65°F (16-18°C).

WATERING (page 8)
 MS - Keep soil moist.
 PD - Let soil become partly dry between waterings.
 DS - Allow soil to dry out between thorough waterings.

Hoya carnosa 'Compacta Mauna Loa'   Hoya carnosa 'Rubra'   Hoya carnosa 'Rubra'

Hoya carnosa 'Compacta Regalis'   Hoya carnosa 'Variegata'   Hoya minata

HOYA (HOY-a)   ML - WA - DS
H. carnosa cultivars (kar-NOH-sa)
Wax Vine, Porcelain Flower, Honey Plant
Evergreen vine with thick, waxy leaves and fragrant blossoms on long flexible stems. Easy, trouble-free plants. Pink to red flower clusters, usually summer and fall. Small or large specimens, for baskets or to climb with support. Grow outdoors in milder climates. Tolerates temperatures as low as 45°F (7°C) for short periods. Grow in general indoor mix; repot infrequently. Propagate from stem cuttings.

'Compacta Mauna Loa' (kom-PAK-ta), **Lura Lei:** natural lei of cream leaves with green edges curling around red stem; flowers light pink.
'Compacta Regalis' (re-GAH-lis), **Hindu Rope;** crinkled deep green leaves with variable creamy borders on red stems. New growth and young leaves deep pink; flowers maroon.
'Rubra' (ROO-bra), **'Krimson Princess':** smooth waxy leaves are variegated with deep pink when young, maturing to cream and green; flowers maroon.
'Variegata' (ve-ri-e-GAH-ta), **Variegated Wax Plant:** strong green leaves with creamy edges, pinkish when young; flowers light pink.

H. minata (mi-NAH-ta)
Rounded velvety leaves and fragrant soft white flowers.

AFTER FLOWERING, leave flowering spurs or stems since next year's blossoms form here. Prefers lower winter temperatures (55°F, 13°C): watering frequency to match slower growth rate. Increase when growth speeds in spring. Flowers initiated in very bright indirect light. Best flower production when pot-bound.
MAINTENANCE Avoid direct hot sun. Fertilize at half recommended strength every 4-8 weeks spring through fall only. Overwatering or poorly drained soil results in root rots. Check for scale insects.

HYACINTHUS (hy-a-SIN-thus)   ML/BL - CA - MS/PD
H. orientalis (o-ree-en-TAH-lis)
Hyacinth
Fragrant-flowered spring bulbs for seasonal indoor decoration. Big, showy clusters of white, pink, red, or blue blossoms rise from center of fresh green leaves. Plant bulbs in pots or bowls, using humusy indoor mix, with tips at or slightly above soil surface. Water thoroughly. Maintain in dark, cool (40-50°F, 5-10°C) place for about 8 weeks until roots are well-developed and shoot tips start to grow. Rewater if soil dries out during this time. After cool period, provide light so leaves can turn green. Move hyacinths to living area when flower starts to emerge. Water to keep soil moist but not soggy. *To flower indoors without soil:* use special hyacinth glass that suspends bulb over water with some charcoal to keep water fresh; replenish water as needed.

Hyacinthus orientalis

Hyacinthus orientalis

Hyacinthus orientalis

Hydrangea

Hypoestes phyllostachya

AFTER FLOWERING, continue regular watering while leaves are green. Plant outdoors in spring; let foliage die back naturally. Varieties that were precooled for early flowering may not flower next spring, but healthy leaves revitalize bulbs for coming seasons.

HYDRANGEA (hy-DRAN-jee-a)　　ML - CA - MS/PD
Snowball Plant
Deciduous flowering shrub for seasonal indoor use. Big flowers in globe-shaped clusters top quilted foliage on woody stems. Flowers last 6-8 weeks in average indoor climates. Fibrous roots. Grow in acid to neutral general indoor mix; repot or plant outdoors in zones 6-7 after flowering. Propagate from stem cuttings.

AFTER FLOWERING, water when soil is partly dry and fertilize every 4-8 weeks through summer. Flower buds form at 60-65°F (16-18°C), develop through dormancy of 6+ weeks total darkness at 40-45°F (5-7°C) or through winter outdoors where hardy (zones 6-7). Blue flowers develop with soil pH about 5.0 (add aluminum sulfate or iron sulfate); pink flowers at pH 6.5 (add lime to reduce soil acidity).

MAINTENANCE Keep soil moist but not soggy while flowering. Prune to shape during dormancy. No fertilizer needed while flowering. Apply acid fertilizer at half recommended rate after flowering. Leach regularly to avoid damaging accumulation of soluble salts. Prefers relative humidity of about 30%. Dry air or drafts cause leaf scorch; dry soil or high salts damage sensitive roots. Check for scale insects.

HYPOESTES (hy-poh-ES-teez)　　ML/BL - WA - PD
H. phyllostachya (fi-loh-STAK-ee-a)
[*H. sanguinolenta* (san-gwi-noh-LEN-ta)]
Polka Dot Plant, Freckle-face
Fast growing tropical herb for warm, somewhat humid places. Pink-speckled foliage, spreading habit. Useful specimen or accent in groups, baskets, dish gardens. Grow in humusy indoor mix; repot or renew plants from stem cuttings every year or two. Several named cultivars.

'Splash', 'Pink Splash': larger rose-pink spots on leaves.

MAINTENANCE Avoid direct scorching sun. Best with minimum night temperature of 60-65°F (16-18°C). Pinch shoot tips to encourage branching and to maintain height at 6-12" (15-30cm). Fertilize at one-quarter recommended strength every 4-8 weeks spring and summer. Reduce watering frequency as growth slows in fall and winter. Best with relative humidity 30% or more. Low light results in spindly growth. Check for whitefly and scale insects.

TO LEACH PLANTS — Water well four or five times in succession, discarding all drainage water. For a more thorough leaching, saturate the soil by immersing the whole container almost to its brim; leave to soak for 10-15 minutes; remove, and allow soil to drain. Repeat several times.

Impatiens hawkeri

Impatiens hawkeri

Impatiens hawkeri

Impatiens wallerana

Impatiens wallerana

Ixora

IMPATIENS (im-PAY-shi-enz)   **BL - CA - MS/PD**

Tender flowering perennial will flower year round with sufficient light. Use as specimen or accent, in hanging baskets, mixed plant groups, on patio or porch, bedding plant outdoors. Slender roots. Easy to grow. Plant in well-draining humusy indoor mix. Grow from seed.
MAINTENANCE Avoid direct scorching sun. Fertilize at half recommended strength every 2-4 weeks spring and summer, less often when growth slows in fall and winter. Trim and prune as desired. Check for spider mites, especially in dry climates.

I. hawkeri hybrids (HAW-ke-ry)
New Guinea Hybrids
Larger, variegated foliage as well as yellow, pink, or white flowers.

I. wallerana (waw-le-RAH-na)
[*I. sultani* (sul-TAH-ny)]
Busy Lizzie, Patience
Green-leaved varieties have brilliantly colorful flowers. Best in diffused bright light, part shade outdoors.

IXORA (ik-SOH-ra)   **BL - WA - H - MS/PD**
Flame-of-the-woods, Jungle Geranium
Tropical evergreen shrub for warm, humid places. Brightly colored flower clusters open from summer on, all year with sufficient light and warmth. Foliage glossy dark green, bronze when young. Accent or specimen; grow outdoors during summer in temperate climates. Grow in acid to neutral indoor mix; repot in late winter or spring. Propagate from stem cuttings.
AFTER FLOWERING, prune to shape and size. Adjust watering and fertilizing frequency to match growth: let soil surface dry between waterings during winter.
MAINTENANCE Keep soil moist but not soggy while flowering. Apply acid fertilizer at half recommended strength every 4-6 weeks spring and summer, less often in fall and winter. Growth becomes spindly in low light. Check for scale insects.

WATERING (page 8)
MS - Keep soil moist.
PD - Let soil become partly dry between waterings.
DS - Allow soil to dry out between thorough waterings.

Kalanchoe blossfeldiana

Kalanchoe blossfeldiana 'Feuerball'

Kalanchoe blossfeldiana 'Melodie'

Kalanchoe fedtschenkoi

Kalanchoe tomentosa

KALANCHOE (ka-LAN-koh-ee)   **BL - WA - DS**

Flowering and foliage succulents provide long-lasting displays. Some develop plantlets on notched leaves. Accents or specimens. Tolerate drought. Fibrous roots. Grow in sandy indoor mix; repot infrequently. Propagate by division, or from plantlets or stem cuttings.
MAINTENANCE Let soil remain dry for longer periods between waterings in winter. Constantly moist soil or poor drainage causes yellow leaves and root losses. Clean plants with gentle spray of water. Fertilize at half recommended strength every month in spring and summer; none in winter. Check for mealybugs.

K. blossfeldiana (blos-fel-dee-AH-na)
Christmas Kalanchoe
Shrubby plants with showy flower clusters and distinctive foliage. Easy to grow.
 AFTER FLOWERING, cut off faded blossoms and trim to shape plant. Continue to water and fertilize through spring and summer. New flower buds form with short days (long nights) and drier soil. Provide at least 14 hours of continuous darkness each night for 12 weeks. Water less during fall dormancy but do not let leaves wilt. Resume normal watering when flower buds swell, or in early spring.
'Feuerball' (FOY-er-bal): compact plant has small dark green leaves and fiery red blossoms.

'Melodie': compact hybrid has large, glossy, scalloped leaves and long-lasting peach blossoms.
'Tom Thumb', Flaming Katy: diminutive dark red flowers and red-tinged foliage.

K. daigramontiana (day-gre-mon-tee-AH-na)
Devil's-backbone
Upright stems with cupped, tooth-edged leaves that produce plantlets along notched margins. Grows to about 36" (90cm).

K. fedtschenkoi (fet-SHEN-koh-ee)
Lavender-scallops, South American Air Plant
Blue-gray leaves bear profuse new plantlets. Pinkish brown bell-shaped flowers in late winter. Sprawling plant grows to height and width 18-36" (45-90cm).

K. manginii (man-JIN-ee-y)
Branching, spreading plant has tiny leaves and tubular red blossoms. Height to about 16" (40cm). Good basket plant.

K. tomentosa (toh-men-TOH-sa)
Pussy-ears, Plush Plant, Panda Plant
Velvety gray leaves with contrasting warm brown edges and tips. Height to about 20" (50cm), spread 12" (30cm).

Lilium: Easter Lily

Leea coccinea

Lilium 'Stargazer'

LEEA (LEE-a) ML - WA - PD
L. coccinea (kok-SIN-ee-a)
Hawaiian Holly, West Indian Holly
Tropical foliage plant for warm, somewhat humid places. Upright habit. Height 3-6' (0.9-1.8m) or more. Large glossy dark green leaves with 4-6" (10-15cm) leaflets. Easy and adaptable. Allow space for natural, uncrowded growth. Tolerates low light. Grow in general indoor mix; repot infrequently. Propagate from main-stem cuttings.

'Burgundy': deeper, richer, leaf color.

MAINTENANCE Avoid direct scorching sun. Fertilize at half recommended strength every 4-6 weeks. Best with relative humidity 30% or more. Clean with periodic spray of tepid water.

LEAF COLOR A GUIDE TO LIGHT NEED
Frequently, the darker-leaved plants—especially those with thick foliage like philodendron and the figs (*Ficus*)— are the ones that grow in low light. Many plants adjust to changing light intensities with new growth to match the available light: leaves become spaced more closely in brighter light, further apart in lower light. Even the leaf cell contents move so that more chlorophyll is exposed in consistently lower light (darker green), and less in brighter light (paler green color).

LILIUM (LIL-i-um) ML - CA - PD
Lily, including **Easter Lily**
Flowering plant for seasonal indoor display. Trumpet blossoms cluster atop leaf-clad stems. Many colors and forms. Grow in sandy indoor mix. Repot when new growth starts after resting period in cool dark place (40-45°F, 5-7°C). Propagate from offsets of fleshy bulbs.
AFTER FLOWERING, trim off dead parts. Continue to water regularly until leaves yellow, then reduce frequency. Fertilize while growth continues at half recommended rate every 4-6 weeks. Keep resting lily bulbs barely damp, not completely dry. Can plant outdoors in spring, allowing leaves to die back naturally. Hardy varieties that have been brought into flower out of season may not flower again the first year, though healthy leaves revitalize bulbs for subsequent years.
MAINTENANCE Best with night minimum 50-55°F (10-13°C) when growing and flowering. Remove anthers before pollen is shed to avoid stained petals, furnishings. No fertilizer needed when flowering. Poor drainage, overwatering result in root rots. Check for botrytis blight, aphids, spider mites.

Liriope muscari

Lithops

Liriope muscari

Liriope muscari 'Variegata'

Lithops

LIRIOPE (li-RY-oh-pay)   **ML/BL - WA - PD**
L. muscari (mus-KAH-ri)
Big Blue Lilyturf

Grass-like foliage plant for warm, somewhat humid indoor use. Blue-purple flowers in summer. Height 12-18" (30-45cm). Specimen or accent, leafy contrast in plant groups. Plant outdoors for ground cover where hardy. Fleshy roots withstand occasional drying out. Spreading tubers. Grow in sandy indoor mix; repot only when potbound. Propagate by division. Named cultivars.
Reported effective in tests to freshen or purify air (page 4).

'Evergreen Giant': taller leafy clusters grow to about 24" (60cm).
'Variegata' (ve-ri-e-GAH-ta), **'Variegated Giant':** yellow striped leaves may burn in strong sunlight.

MAINTENANCE Needs bright indirect light for flower development; avoid direct scorching sun. Best with night minimum 50-55°F (10-13°C). Trim off dead flowers, damaged leaves and leaf-tips. Fertilize at half recommended rate every 4-8 weeks. Leach regularly to avoid damaging accumulation of soluble salts. Best with relative humidity 30% or more. Dry air and drafts cause leaf burn. Fluorides in soil and/or water may cause leaflet margin damage. Check for scale insects.

LITHOPS (LITH-ops)   **BL - WA - DS**
Living Stones

Unusual tiny succulents blend with surrounding stones in their native desert areas of South Africa. Each plant is a pair of modified leaves that splits apart with new growth in spring; older pair remains through growing season. Height 2-3" (5-10cm); plant spreads slowly, forming clump. White or yellow daisy-like flowers cover leaves in fall. Grow on bright windowsill or in other location where light is strong. Very slow growing. Long tap root. Plant permanently in very sandy indoor mix. Propagate from seed or by division.
MAINTENANCE   Water lightly when soil is dry, or let established living stones absorb water from saucer. Soil must dry out between waterings. Plants become dormant as older leaf pairs die out; during dormancy, water infrequently if at all. Fertilize rarely, at 1/4 recommended strength no more than once or twice each year, in spring and summer. Although naturally they grow buried with only flat tops showing, container-grown living stones are best planted with leaves exposed to prevent rotting.

Livistona chinensis

Mammillaria elongata

Lygodium japonicum

LIVISTONA (li-vis-TON-a)   ML/BL - CA - MS
Fan Palm
L. chinensis (chi-NEN-sis)
Chinese Fan Palm, Chinese Fountain Palm
Tropical fan palm has rounded, fringed fronds 3-6' (0.9-1.8m) across.
Young plants for containers; larger specimens for interiorscapes, malls.
Grow in well-draining, rich, humusy palm mix. Propagate from seed.
MAINTENANCE In winter, let soil become partly dry between water-
ings. Wipe leaves or wash with water to remove dust. Fertilize every
month spring through fall. Trim damaged and discolored foliage. Check
for spider mites and scale insects.

LYGODIUM (ly-GOH-di-um)   ML - CA - H - PD
Climbing Fern
L. japonicum (ja-PON-i-kum)
Japanese Climbing Fern
Dainty, delicate fern for moist atmospheres. Yellow-green foliage on
long twining stems. Fast growing. Rhizomes and fibrous roots. Grow
in pots or baskets with humusy indoor or basic fern mix. Propagate
by division when repotting in spring.
MAINTENANCE Mist with plain water to clean foliage; avoid chemicals. Fertilize at one-quarter recommended strength every 4-6 weeks,
or with weaker solution at every watering while growth is active. As
growth slows, reduce watering, stop fertilizing, and set plant in cooler area. Leaf edges turn brown in dry air. Check for slugs and snails
on plants moved in from shade outdoors, and for spider mites, mealybugs, and scale insects.

MAMMILLARIA (ma-mi-LAH-ri-a)   BL - WA/CA - DS
Pincushion, Strawberry Cactus
Wide range of rounded and columnar cacti with single or clustered
stems in many sizes. Height 2-6" (5-15cm) indoors. Spines soft or
sharp. Flowers open in ring around top of stem. Includes some of the
easiest cacti. Tolerant of drought. Grow in sandy indoor mix. Propagate
from seed or stem cuttings of columnar forms.
MAINTENANCE Provide warm temperatures when growing and cool
when dormant, usually in winter. Keep completely dry in winter; plant
rots easily. Fertilize at half recommended strength every month, spring
and summer. Rotting results from overwatering or excess humidity.

M. elongata (e-lon-GAH-ta)
Lace Cactus, Golden-star Cactus, Gold Lace Cactus, Ladyfinger
Clustering cylinders have curved golden spines, white flowers in spring.
Easy to grow.

Maranta leuconeura var. *erythroneura*

Maranta leuconeura

Maranta leuconeura var. *kerchoveana*

Melissa officinalis: lemon balm

M. plumosa (ploo-MOH-sa)
Feather Cactus
Cluster of rounded green stems covered with feathery white spines. Creamy flowers in midwinter. Add limestone to soil to reduce acidity.

MARANTA (ma-RAN-ta) ML - WA - H - MS/PD
M. leuconeura varieties (loo-koh-NEW-ra)
Prayer Plant
Tropical foliage plants with leaves that fold up at night. Spreading stems; height 4-8" (10-20cm). Characteristic foliage markings, undersides often red. Tiny flowers. Accent, basket, dish garden plant. Fibrous roots. Grow in well-draining humusy indoor mix; repot infrequently. Propagate by division and from stem cuttings.

M. l. var. *erythroneura* (e-rith-roh-NEW-ra)
Red-nerve Plant, Red-veined Prayer Plant
Rose-red veins and dark markings on olive green leaves with red-purple undersides.

M. l. var. *kerchoveana* (ker-choh-vee-AH-na)
Green Maranta, Rabbit Tracks
Gray-green leaves with red-brown rabbit tracks that mature dark green.

M. l. var. *leuconeura*
[*M. l.* var. *massangeana* (ma-san-jee-AH-na)]
Massange's Arrowroot
Leaves have wine red undersides, red veins.
MAINTENANCE Best with night temperature above 65°F (18°C). Let soil dry more between waterings in winter. Pinch back leggy growth to maintain shape. Clean with gentle spray of tepid water. Fertilize at half recommended strength every 4-8 weeks while growing rapidly. Trim damaged and dead leaves. Fluorides in soil and/or water may cause leaflet margin damage. Check for spider mites.

MELISSA (me-LIS-a) BL - CA - MS
M. officinalis (o-fi-si-NAH-lis)
Lemon Balm
Vigorous, perennial, lemon-flavored mint. Height indoors about 12" (30cm). Inconspicuous white flowers. Growing tips and leaves flavor sauces, fish, meats, salads, fruit dishes, tea and cool drinks. Grow from seed, stem cuttings, or divisions in individual container with general indoor mix. Invasive rhizomes crowd others out of group planting.
MAINTENANCE Harvest or pinch back regularly to encourage bushiness. Fertilize at half recommended strength every 2-4 weeks when growth is vigorous; every 4-8 weeks during winter.

Melocactus matanzanus

Monstera deliciosa

Mentha: mint

Narcissus

MELOCACTUS (me-loh-KAK-tus)   BL - WA - DS
Turk's-cap
M. matanzanus (mah-tan-ZAH-nus)
Dwarf Turk's-cap

Rounded, ribbed, cactus has short curving spines whose red coloring becomes yellowish with age. Permanent woolly cap called cephalium develops in 4-5 years at top of dark green stem. Pink flowers form in this cap. Tolerates less strong light than many other cacti. Rarely needs repotting. Grow in sandy indoor mix.

MAINTENANCE   Provide warm temperatures all year. Water somewhat less frequently in winter and in lower light conditions. Fertilize at half recommended strength every month in spring and summer. Rotting can result from overwatering and excess humidity.

MENTHA (MEN-tha)   BL - CA - MS
Mint

Several differently flavored, vigorous perennial leafy herbs. Flowers inconspicuous. Growing tips and leaves used for flavoring sauces, cool drinks, salads, desserts, and as garnishes. Grow from seed, stem cuttings, or divisions, in individual container with general indoor mix. Invasive rhizomes quickly fill group planter.

MAINTENANCE   Harvest or trim back regularly to contain height and encourage bushiness. Fertilize at half recommended strength every 2-4 weeks when growth is vigorous; every 4-8 weeks during winter.

MONSTERA (mon-STEH-ra, mon-STEE-ra)   ML/LL - WA - PD
M. deliciosa (dee-li-si-OH-sa)
Splitleaf Philodendron, Swiss-cheese Plant, Hurricane Plant

Durable jungle vine with large perforated and split leaves that gleam like polished leather. Easy and adaptable. Allow space for natural, uncrowded growth; provide support for heavy vine. Tolerates low light and occasionally dry soil. Plant in general indoor mix; repot infrequently. Propagate from stem cuttings and by air-layering.

MAINTENANCE   Avoid direct scorching sun. Let soil dry out more between waterings in winter. Fertilize at half recommended strength every 4-6 weeks during spring and summer, every 6-8 weeks in fall and winter. Drafts result in leaf burn. Overwatering can cause yellowed leaves. Rejuvenate leggy plants by air-layering or heavy pruning. Check for spider mites, mealybugs, and scale insects.

NARCISSUS (nar-SIS-us)   BL - CA - MS/PD
Daffodils, Narcissi

Flowering bulbs for seasonal indoor decoration. Large and small trumpet flowers mainly in yellows, creams, and white. Easy to grow. Plant

Narcissus

Nematanthus 'Tropicana'

Narcissus tazetta 'Paperwhite'

Nematanthus wettsteinii

bulbs in pots or bowls, using humusy indoor mix, with tips at or slightly above soil surface. Water thoroughly. Keep planted bulbs dark and cool (35-40°F, 2-5°C) for about 8 weeks until roots are well-developed and 2-4" (5-10cm) top growth is showing. Rewater if soil dries out during this time. After cool period, provide light so leaves can turn green, and move to warmer place for flower development. Do not fertilize.

To flower indoors without soil, anchor bulbs between pebbles at top of pebble-and-water-filled bowl so just lower bulb edges touch water. Replenish water as needed.

AFTER FLOWERING, continue to water to maintain leaves. Plant outdoors in spring; let foliage die back naturally. Varieties that were forced into early flowering may not flower well next spring, but healthy leaves revitalize bulbs for coming seasons.

NEMATANTHUS (ne-ma-TAN-thus)　　BL - WA - H - PD
[*Hypocyrta* (hy-poh-KUR-ta)]

Shrubby epiphytic gesneriads with trailing or upright stems. Small, unequally paired, smooth, glossy leaves. Tubular flowers in shades of red, orange or pink, on slender stems. Blooms from spring to summer, longer in well-lighted locations. Shallow fibrous roots. Grow in acid soil (pH 6.0-7.0), using basic gesneriad mix. Repot infrequently. Propagate from stem cuttings or by division.

AFTER FLOWERING, trim more vigorous plants to desired shape and size. Water less often as growth slows, and maintain dormant plants without fertilizer until new leaves expand in spring. Flower buds form on new season's growth.

MAINTENANCE Shade from strong sun in summer and outdoors. Avoid extreme heat; stem rot can develop above 85°F (30°C). Spray or mist with water to clean. Apply high phosphate fertilizer at half recommended strength every 3-6 weeks while growing vigorously, every 6-12 weeks when growth slows in fall and winter; none while dormant. Cut off dying flowers, discolored foliage. Dry and cool air causes premature flower drop. Both fully dry and constantly wet soil cause root loss. Leach regularly to avoid salts damage to delicate roots. White and brown dead areas on leaves can indicate sun-scorch. Check for spider mites, scale insects, whitefly, and mealybugs.

N. 'Tropicana', Tropicana Pouch Flower: spreading and upright habit. Dark, shiny leaves, striped and spotted yellow-orange flowers.

N. wettsteinii (wet-STY-nee-y)
Goldfish Plant, Miniature Pouch Flower
Diminutive waxy leaves; vibrant orange blossoms with bright yellow tips. Good basket plant.

Neoregelia 'Fireball'

Noeregelia carolinae 'Tricolor'

Neoregelia carolinae 'Tricolor'

NEOREGELIA (nee-oh-re-GEL-i-a)   **ML - WA - MS**

Blushing bromeliads develop brilliant, long-lasting red or purple centers when flowers form. Tolerates some full sun and full shade. Best color in bright indirect light or intermittent full sun. Flower clusters held close to center of multicolored rosette. Small, fleshy root system; established plants rarely need repotting. Grow in porous, slightly acid bromeliad mix. Propagate from offsets.

Reported effective in tests to freshen or purify air (page 4).

AFTER FLOWERING, young plants, or offsets, grow at plant base. When at least one-third the size of parent, cut from mature parent plant and pot separately.

MAINTENANCE Keep water in central cup at all times. Clean upper leaf surfaces gently with moist soft cloth. Fertilize at one-quarter recommended strength, applied to soil and cup every 4 weeks. Provide relative humidity 30% or more; brown leaf tips indicate dry air. Trim damaged, discolored parts. Check for scale insects; avoid use of oil sprays to prevent damage to food-absorbing tissues.

***N.* 'Argenta':** ivory-edged leaves develop pink center at flowering. Produces many offsets.

***N.* 'Fireball':** clustering, short-leaved rosettes that become more red with stronger light. Each rosette spreads 5-8" (13-20cm), is borne on long stem or stolon.

N. carolinae (ka-roh-LIN-ee)
Blushing Bromeliad

Dark green rosette center blushes bright red for flowering. Many offsets develop after flowering.

'Flandria': cream-edged green leaves in formal rosette whose center turns deep pink at flowering.

'Tricolor' (TRY-co-lor), **Striped Blushing Bromeliad:** rose, ivory, and green stripes. Crimson center at flowering may last 12 months.

'Tricolor Perfecta' (per-FEK-ta): crisp ivory and green stripes, rose-crimson center.

NEPHROLEPIS (nef-roh-LEP-is)   **ML/BL - CA - H - PD**
Sword Fern

Tropical and subtropical ferns for airy, humid indoor climates. Variable, divided fronds with scaly stems. Small or large specimen or accent for table, pedestal, or basket; contrast for dish garden or group planting. Fast growing. Short rhizomes, fibrous roots. Repot infrequently, using humusy indoor or basic fern mix. Propagate by division.

MAINTENANCE Best with diffused bright light to partial shade; sun in winter. Cut older fronds back to soil level to encourage fresh new

Nephrolepis exaltata 'Dallas'

Nephrolepis exaltata 'Bostoniensis'

Nephrolepis exaltata 'Bostoniensis Compacta'

Nephrolepis exaltata 'Florida Ruffle'

Nephrolepis exaltata 'Fluffy Ruffles'

growth. Fertilize at one-quarter recommended strength every 4-6 weeks, or with weaker solution at every watering while growth is active. Roots can be damaged by stronger applications. As growth slows reduce watering and fertilizing frequency. Spray with water occasionally, only to clean foliage. Do not mist regularly; sensitive to chlorine and other chemicals. Foliage and roots rot in wet conditions. Check for slugs and snails on plants moved in from shade outdoors, and for scale insects, mealybugs, spider mites.

N. biserrata **'Furcans'** (by-se-RAH-ta FUR-kanz)
Fishtail Fern, Purplestalk Sword Fern
Dark green fronds with widely spaced leaflets that have forked, fishtail-like tips. Fronds grow to 4' (1.2m).

N. cordifolia **'Plumosa'** (kor-di-FOH-li-a ploo-MOH-sa)
Dwarf Whitman Fern
Bright green, arching fronds grow to about 2½' (75cm).

N. duffii (DUF-ee-y)
[*N. cordifolia* 'Duffii']
Pygmy Sword Fern
Tiny rounded leaflets line each side of 2' (60cm), very narrow fronds.

N. exaltata cultivars (ek-sal-TAH-ta)
'Bostoniensis': Boston Fern: arching and trailing fresh green fronds, 2-5' (0.6-1.5m) long.
'Bostoniensis Compacta' ['Compacta'] ((kom-PAK-ta), **Dwarf Boston Fern:** shorter fronds, more upright habit.
'Dallas' ['Dallas Jewel']: dense, clustered fronds.
'Florida Ruffle': dense ruffles on thickly clustered fronds 18-24" (45-60cm) long.
'Fluffy Ruffles', Dwarf Feather Fern: upright, dark green fronds about 12" (30cm) long.
'Hillsii', Crisped Feather Fern: long, narrow, upright to trailing fronds have crisply undulating leaflets.
'Mini-Ruffle': upright, compact 2-3" (5-8cm) fronds.
'Petticoat', Boston Petticoat: long arched and trailing fronds have frilled and ruffled leaflets.
'Rooseveltii', Roosevelt Fern: long, fresh green fronds have wavy, lobed leaflets.
'Teddy Jr.': compact dwarf form with narrow yellow-green wavy fronds.
'Verona', Verona Lace Fern: long, trailing fronds with lacy leaflets give plant feathery look.
Additional cultivars: **'Kimberly', 'Maasil'.**

Nidularium billbergioides

Notocactus haselbergii

Notocactus leninghausii

Nidularium innocentii var. lineatum

Nidularium innocentii

NIDULARIUM (ni-dew-LAH-ri-um)   **LL/ML - WA - MS**

Low-growing bromeliads with smooth, glossy leaves. Flowering clusters among large colorful bracts at rosette centers. Small, fleshy root systems; established plants rarely need repotting. Grow in porous, slightly acid bromeliad mix. Propagate spring to summer from offsets. AFTER FLOWERING, young plants or offsets grow at plant base. When at least one-third the size of parent, cut off and pot separately.

MAINTENANCE Keep water in central cup at all times. Let soil dry slightly in winter. Clean upper surface of foliage gently with moist soft cloth. Fertilize at one-quarter recommended strength, applied to soil and cup, every 4 weeks. Provide relative humidity of 30% or more; brown leaf tips indicate dry air. Trim damaged, discolored parts. Check for scale insects, mealybugs, and basal rot.

N. billbergioides (bil-ber-jee-OI-deez)
[*N. citrinum* (sit-REE-num)]
Small green rosette spreads to 12" (30cm) across. At flowering, rosette center turns yellow.

N. innocentii varieties (i-no-SEN-tee-y)
Strap-like leaves grow to 12" (30cm) long. White flowers.
N. i. var. innocentii, Black Amazonian Birdnest: dark red coloring

mostly under leaves. Bracts in flower cluster are red.
N. i. var. lineatum (li-nee-AH-tum), **Lined Birdnest:** green-and-white striped leaves with maroon-tipped central bracts. Richer soil results in more green coloring.

NOTOCACTUS (no-toh-KAK-tus)   **BL - WA/CA - DS**
[*Parodia* (pa-ROH-di-a)]
Ball Cactus

Rounded to columnar, densely spiny cacti have clustered or single stems. Easy to grow. Young plants often flower indoors. Slow growing. Plant in sandy indoor mix.

MAINTENANCE Provide warm temperatures when growing and cool when dormant, usually in winter. Water sparingly during dormancy. Fertilize at half recommended strength every month in spring and summer. Rotting can result from overwatering and excess humidity.

N. haselbergii (ha-sel-BER-jee-y)
Scarlet Ball Cactus
Red flowers cluster on flattened top of globular 3-4" (8-10cm) high stem. Silvery white spines.

N. leninghausii (le-ning-HOW-zee-y)
Golden Ball Cactus

Notocactus scopa

Oncidium

Ocimum basilicum: sweet basil

Oncidium

Clustering columnar stems with golden spines. Yellow flowers on small woolly crown at stem top. Grows to height of 2-3' (60-90cm).

N. scopa (SKOH-pa)
Silver Ball Cactus
Rounded to columnar clustered stems have dense silvery outer spines, and red or yellow-brown central spines in each group. Flowers yellow. Height 10-18" (25-45cm).

OCIMUM (oh-SEE-mum)   **BL - CA - PD**
O. basilicum cultivars (ba-SIL-i-kum)
Common Sweet Basil
Annual aromatic herb in a variety of flavors and colors. Bright, shiny leaves and white flowers. Height indoors can be held to about 12" (30cm). Chopped leaves are fine addition to raw and cooked tomatoes. Flavor intensifies with cooking: add to soups, stews, sauces, cheese and egg dishes, meats, fish, poultry, and salads. Sow seed or pot young plants in general indoor mix.
MAINTENANCE Harvest or pinch back regularly to encourage bushiness, maintain leafy development, and prevent flowering. Fertilize at half recommended strength every 2-4 weeks when growth is vigorous; every 4-8 weeks during winter.

ONCIDIUM (on-SID-ee-um)   **ML - WA - H - DS**
Dancing-lady Orchid, Butterfly Orchid, Dancing-doll Orchid
Tropical orchids bear long clusters of fragrant, colorful, dainty blossoms. Clustered short leaves rise in pairs from swollen stems or pseudobulbs. Grow with shade outdoors in summer. Epiphytic: mount to hang in humid greenhouse climate. Indoors, plant in small containers with well-draining, moisture retaining mix containing both fibrous and water-holding materials or use ready-made epiphytic orchid mix. Reduce depth of growing medium with deep underlayer of clean broken pot. Repot in spring every few years to renew soil. Propagate by division into smaller clusters, each with three or more pseudobulbs. AFTER FLOWERING and when growth slows, reduce watering and fertilizing frequency. When new growth starts, resume regular applications.
MAINTENANCE Avoid direct scorching sun in summer. Best with minimum night temperatures 50-60°F (10-16°C), and days 75-80°F (24-27°C). While growing, water thoroughly as soon as soil is dry. Fertilize every 2-4 weeks while growing. Root rot results from poor drainage, overwatering. Dark leaves and soft new growth result from insufficient light. Check for slugs and snails on outdoor orchids, and indoors for spider mites, scale insects, mealybugs, rots, and leafspot.

Opuntia aoracantha

Opuntia microdasys var. *rufida*

Opuntia subulata

Opuntia microdasys

Opuntia macrocentra

OPUNTIA (o-PUN-ti-a)   BL - WA/CA - DS
Prickly Pear, Tuna, Cholla Cactus

Low and spreading or small tree-like cacti often have jointed stems; stem sections called pads are either flat ("tuna") or cylindrical ("cholla"). Many pads are dotted with characteristic clusters of bristles and spines. Showy though short-lived groups. Fast growing. Grow in sandy indoor mix. Propagate from stem sections, cuttings, or seed. Glochids (bristly clusters) of many prickly pear cacti have many easily detached barbed bristles that cling to the skin until removed, usually in warm or hot soapy water.

MAINTENANCE Provide warm temperatures when growing and cool when dormant, usually in winter. Water sparingly during dormancy. Fertilize at half recommended strength every month from spring to fall. Rotting can result from overwatering and excess humidity.

O. aoracantha (ay-o-ra-KAN-tha)
[*O. paediophylla* (pay-dee-oh-FIL-a)]
Paper Spine
Gray-green stem has flexible 2-8" (5-20cm) gray spines.

O. clavarioides (kla-va-ree-OI-deez)
Crested Opuntia, Sea-coral, Fairy-castles, Gnome's-throne
Branching, cylindrical branches in contorted cluster. Often grafted.

O. leucotricha (loo-koh-TRIK-a)
Tree-like form with oval pads and yellow glochids.

O. macrocentra (mak-roh-SEN-tra)
[*O. violacea* var. *macrocentra* (vy-oh-LAY-see-a)]
Black-spined Prickly Pear
Rounded to oval pads with spiny margins. Distinct black spines.

O. microdasys (mik-roh-DAZ-is)
Bunny-ears, Rabbit-ears, Goldplush
Shrubby, sprawling flat-jointed cactus with spineless golden glochids in diagonal lines. Height to about 12" (15cm) in container.
O. m. var. *rufida* [*O. rufida* (ROO-fi-da)], **Cinnamon Cactus, Blind Pear, Red Bunny-ears:** Red glochids on elongated joints or pads.

O. monacantha (mo-na-KAN-tha)
[*O. vulgaris* (vul-GAH-ris)]
Prickly Pear, Barbary Fig, Irish-mittens
Shrubby cactus with thin, flat pads about 12" (30cm) long. One or two 1-1$^{1}/_{2}$" (2.5-4cm) spines extend from each brown glochid.

O. subulata (soo-bew-LAH-ta)
Eve's Pin Cactus
Tree-like, branching shrub with long cylindrical joints. Small pin or needle-shaped leaves persist. Few spines or glochids.

Origanum: marjoram, oregano

Oxalis

Oxalis

Pachypodium lamerei

ORIGANUM (o-ree-GAH-num)   BL - CA - PD
Sweet Marjoram, Marjoram, Oregano
O. majorana (mar-jo-RAH-na)
O. vulgare (vul-GAH-ree)
Compact, slow-growing bushy perennial herbs with gray-green or dark leaves. Pinch to contain height at about 8" (20cm). Chop leaves to flavor meats, fish, poultry, soups, stews, salads, and egg and cheese dishes. Sow seed direct, take root cuttings, or pot young plants in general indoor mix.
MAINTENANCE Fertilize at half recommended strength every 2-4 weeks when growth is vigorous; every 4-8 weeks during winter. Cut stems to dry when flower buds form. Continue to water roots as needed, and resume fertilizing when new shoots appear.

OXALIS (ok-SAH-lis)   ML/BL - CA - PD/DS
Oxalis, Shamrock
Friendly flowering plants with shamrock leaves. Easily grown small or larger specimens for table, hanging basket. White or pink flowers open in winter and spring, all year with sufficient light. Grow in well-draining indoor mix; repot when rootbound. Propagate by division.
AFTER FLOWERING, leaves may die down. Bulbs or tubers benefit from rest in drier soil and at cooler temperatures (50°F, 10°C). Repot

and divide as needed. New growth resumes with increased watering and resumed fertilizer applications.
MAINTENANCE Avoid direct scorching sun. Let soil dry out between waterings when plant is resting. Trim off dead parts. Fertilize at half recommended strength every 3-6 weeks while growing. Check for spider mites.

PACHYPODIUM (pa-ki-POH-di-um)   BL - WA - DS
P. lamerei (LAY-me-ry)
Madagascar Palm, Club Foot
Spiny succulent has upright single trunk 2-6' (0.6-1.8m) high with pinkish 1-1½" (2.5-4cm) spines. Palm-like plant has swollen base, is topped with cluster of dark green, strap-shaped leaves 5-8" (13-20cm) long. Leaves have white midribs. White flowers rare in container-grown plants. Unusual specimen or accent. Grow in sandy indoor mix; repot infrequently. Propagate from seed.
MAINTENANCE Water sparingly during dormancy which may be during summer. Fertilize at half recommended strength every 2 months while growing. Constantly moist soil or poor drainage causes yellow leaves and root losses.

91

Pachystachys lutea

Paphiopedilum

Pelargonium peltatum

PACHYSTACHYS (pa-ki-STAK-is)   ML - WA - H - MS
P. lutea (LOO-tee-a)
Gold Hops, Lollipops
Tropical flowering shrub grows 12-36" (30-90cm). Bright green quilted leaves topped by 3-6" (8-15cm) spikes of golden bracts that outlive slender white blossoms. Flowers in warm weather, year round in good light. Grow in general indoor mix. Propagate from stem cuttings.
AFTER FLOWERING, cut off faded flower heads. Let soil dry more between waterings and reduce fertilizing frequency to match growth rate. Repot if needed before new flush of growth. Prune as needed.
MAINTENANCE Shade from direct sun in summer; provide cool direct sun in winter. Keep soil moist but not soggy and fertilize at half recommended strength during growing and flowering. Leach regularly to avoid damaging accumulation of soluble salts. Roots rot in poorly drained or cool, wet soil. Check for spider mites and whitefly.

PAPHIOPEDILUM (pa-fee-oh-PED-i-lum)   ML - CA - H - PD
Lady-slipper Orchid, Venus'-slipper, Cypripedium
Temperate climate orchids with long-lasting 2-4" (5-10cm) blossoms usually borne singly. Many colors and combinations of speckled, mottled or striped glossy flowers. Distinctive pouched lip. Foliage is rosette of leathery, strap-shaped leaves, smooth green or mottled. Green leaf

forms generally flower in winter or spring, and prefer cool climate; grow outdoors in warmer areas. Mottled leaf forms generally flower in spring or summer, and prefer average climate. One of the easiest of indoor orchids. Fine fibrous root system. Grow in small containers with humusy indoor mix or sphagnum moss plus sandy loam. Repot in spring every few years to renew soil. Propagate by division.
MAINTENANCE Bright indirect light in winter, part shade or diffused light at other times. Excess light inhibits flowering, causes yellowed foliage. Let soil dry more between waterings while plant rests in winter. Fertilize every 2-4 weeks while growing. Check for slugs and snails on outdoor orchids, and for spider mites, scale insects, mealybugs, rots, and leafspot on those indoors.

PELARGONIUM (pe-lar-GON-i-um)   BL - CA - DS/PD
Geranium
Versatile flowering plants for indoors and out. Growth continues year round in good light. Many cultivars have prolific colorful blossoms all summer; others have scented foliage. Various forms include *ivy, regal, scented,* and *zonal* geraniums. Grow in well-draining general indoor mix. Repot in late winter. Propagate from stem cuttings and seed.
AFTER FLOWERING, reduce watering and fertilizing frequency as growth slows. Leaves die back if light is too low: store roots dry, in or

Pelargonium X *domesticum*　　　　*Pelargonium graveolens*　　　　*Pelargonium graveolens*

Pelargonium peltatum

Pellaea rotundifolia

out of soil, in cool frost-free place. Or cut plants back and maintain nearly dry through winter. Growth starts with added water in brighter, longer days; resume fertilizing when first leaves expand.

MAINTENANCE Fertilize at half recommended strength every 4 weeks during rapid growth. Trim regularly to remove faded leaves and blossoms; prune to shape as needed. Distorted, misshapen leaves caused by virus infections: separate and discard affected plants. Wet soil and continually moist conditions result in bacterial rots. Check for whitefly, aphids, mealybugs.

P. X*domesticum* (do-MES-ti-kum)　　　　　　　　　　**MS/PD**
Fancy Geranium, Martha Washington Geranium, Regal Geranium
Show geraniums prefer moist though not soggy soil during growth and flowering, with cool days (65°F, 18°C).

P. *graveolens* (gra-VEE-oh-lenz)
Rose Geranium, Sweet-scented Geranium
Foliage fragrances include rose, lemon, mint, pine, and spices.

P. X*hortorum* (hor-TOR-um)
Zonal, Bedding Geranium
Familiar summer bedding plants for bright indoor locations. Many varieties have distinct zones of dark green or red-purple on leaves.

P. *peltatum* (pel-TAH-tum)
Ivy Geranium, Ivy-leaved Geranium
Smooth ivy-shaped leaves on vigorous trailing plant. Flowers continuously all summer. Excellent basket plant. Best with relative humidity 30% or more.

PELLAEA (pe-LEE-a)　　　　　　　　　　**ML/BL - CA - PD**
P. *rotundifolia* (roh-tun-di-FOH-li-a)
Button Fern
Warm-temperate xerophytic fern grows outdoors in mild areas. Low and spreading, with deep green round to oval leaflets on 12" (30cm) fronds. Stems brown-black. Accent, contrast, basket plant. Easily grown; tolerates drier air than most ferns. Fast growing. Spreading rhizomes. Plant in shallow container like half-pot or azalea pot, or reduce soil depth with deep under-layer of broken clean pot. Plant in humusy indoor or basic fern mix. Repot as needed. Propagate by division.

MAINTENANCE Best with diffused bright light to partial shade; moderate sun in winter. Protect from drafts. Cut older fronds back to soil level to encourage fresh new growth. Spray with tepid water to clean. Fertilize at one-quarter recommended strength every 4-6 weeks spring and summer. Best with relative humidity 30% or more; wilts quickly when too dry.

Peperomia argyreia

Peperomia caperata 'Emerald Ripple'

Pellionia repens

PELLIONIA (pe-lee-ON-i-a)   **LL/ML - WA - PD/MS**

Tropical small foliage plant for warm, somewhat humid climates. Spreading, trailing, branching stems, attractively patterned foliage. Use in hanging basket, as groundcover, in dish gardens, terrariums. Slow growing. Grow in humusy indoor mix; repot infrequently. Propagate from stem cuttings, planting several to a pot, or divisions.
MAINTENANCE Let soil dry more between waterings in winter. Prune overgrown stems and pinch long stem tips to encourage branching. Fertilize at half recommended strength every 3-6 weeks in spring and summer only. Best with relative humidity 30% or more. Avoid drafts and dry air which cause leaf burn. Overwatering, soggy soil, and drought result in leaf drop. Check for spider mites.

P. pulchra (PUL-kra)
Satin Pellionia
Distinctive dark veins on close-set foliage; pinkish stems.

P. repens (REE-penz)
[*P. daveauana* (da-voh-AH-na)]
Trailing Watermelon Begonia
Purple-tinted leaves have dark area along each side.

PEPEROMIA (pe-pe-ROM-i-a)   **ML - WA - PD**

Small bushy foliage plants for table or desk, dish garden, windowsill, hanging basket. Distinctive markings on heavy, waxy leaves. Slender flowering spikes may rise above foliage. Easy to grow, adaptable. Upright or prostrate habit. Tolerate low light for short periods. Grow in well-draining general indoor mix. Propagate by division and from leaf cuttings or stem cuttings.
MAINTENANCE Avoid full sun. Let soil dry more between waterings when growth is slow in winter. Fertilize at half recommended strength every 8 weeks spring through fall. Leach regularly to avoid damaging accumulation of soluble salts. Trim off damaged, yellowed leaves. Overwatering results in root rot, yellowed leaves. Check for spider mites, mealybugs.

P. argyreia (ar-gy-REE-a)
[*P. sandersii* (SAN-der-see-y)]
Watermelon Peperomia
Silver and blue-green patterned leaves on red stems.

P. caperata 'Emerald Ripple' (ka-pe-RAH-ta)
Masses of quilted dark green leaves on red stems. Height 3-4" (8-10cm).

Peperomia obtusifolia

Peperomia scandens 'Variegata' (young plant)

Peperomia rotundifolia

Petroselinum crispum: parsley

P. obtusifolia (ob-tew-si-FOH-li-a)
Pepper Face, Baby Rubber Plant
Like a miniature India rubber plant, smooth leaves are dark green, faintly cupped. Upright stems bow under weight of foliage.
'Variegata' (ve-ri-e-GAH-ta), **Variegated Peperomia:** creamy variegations on smooth foliage.

P. orba (OR-ba)
Princess Astrid
Low spreading species with dark green, short-stemmed leaves.

P. rotundifolia (roh-tun-di-FOH-li-a)
[*P. nummulariifolia* (nu-mew-lah-ree-i-FOH-li-a)]
Trailing Peperomia
Slim stems with small elliptical green leaves; longer shoots trail. Easy.
P. r.* var. *pilosior (py-LOH-zee-or) [*P. prostrata*], **Prostrate Peperomia:** rounded, red-edged leaves on slender trailing stems.

***P. scandens* 'Variegata'** (SKAN-denze)
Cupid Peperomia
Trails of fleshy green-and-cream leaves on pale stems that become tinged red in light. Easy to grow.

P. verschaffeltii (ver-sha-FEL-tee-y)
[*P. marmorata* (mar-mor-RAH-ta)]
Sweetheart Peperomia
Heart-shaped foliage has silver banding on green or blue-green leaves.

PETROSELINUM (pet-ro-se-LEE-num) BL - CA - PD
P. crispum (KRIS-pum)
Parsley
Fragrant biennial herb best grown as annual. Finely divided foliage is curled (**var. *crispum***) or flattish (**var. *neapolitanum*, Italian Parsley**). Use leaves, fresh or dried, for garnish and in meat, fish, poultry, vegetable, and egg dishes as well as in soups, salads, and sauces. Trim often to maintain height of about 8" (20cm). Seed slow to germinate. Grow from seed or seedlings each year in general indoor mix. Fibrous roots thicken with age. Sturdy outdoor-grown roots can be brought indoors in moist sand, to provide fresh leaves during winter.
MAINTENANCE Fertilize indoor-grown plants at half recommended strength every 2-4 weeks when growth is vigorous, every 4-8 weeks through winter.

Phalaenopsis 'Show Girl'   Phalaenopsis stuartina   Phalaenopsis 'Kistler'

Philodendron 'Emerald King'   Philodendron 'Emerald Queen'

PHALAENOPSIS (fay-le-NOP-sis)   ML/BL - WA - H - MS
Moth Orchid

Tropical orchids have broad, leathery, spreading, 12" (30cm) leaves. Flower clusters grow to 36" (90cm), individual flowers 3-6" (8-15cm) wide, flattish; wide upper petals. Colors white, cream, yellow, lavender, pink, may have contrasting lip or spots. Epiphytic: mount to hang in warm, humid greenhouse climate. For indoor containers use well-draining, moisture retaining mix of fibrous and water-holding materials: osmunda, coarsely shredded fir bark, redwood chips, or small pumice stones with coarse peat moss and/or perlite. Or use ready-made epiphytic orchid mix. Reduce depth of soil with underlayer of clean broken pot. Repot in spring every few years to renew soil. Propagate from stem cuttings, using rooting lateral branches.
MAINTENANCE Prefer brighter light in late fall and winter, though avoid direct sun at all times. Best with nights above 60°F (16°C). Let soil become partly dry between waterings in winter when plant grows more slowly. Fertilize every 2-4 weeks spring through summer, every 4-8 weeks in fall and winter. Or spray with dilute fertilizer solution every 1-2 weeks when growth is rapid. Root rot results from poor drainage, overwatering. Dark leaves and soft new growth result from insufficient light. Check for slugs and snails on outdoor orchids, and indoors for spider mites, scale insects, mealybugs, rots, and leafspot.

PHILODENDRON (fi-lo-DEN-dron)   ML/LL - CA/WA - PD

Versatile and adaptable tropical foliage with variously shaped and colored leaves. Most are epiphytic vines. Specimen, in groups, baskets. Tolerates very low light and cool to warm indoor climates. Fleshy roots grow easily from stems, withstand occasional drought. Grow in general or well-draining humusy indoor mix. Repot infrequently. Propagate from stem cuttings, and by air-layering larger plants.
Reported effective in tests to freshen or purify air (page 4).
MAINTENANCE Let soil dry more between waterings in winter. Provide support for vining philodendrons, or space for them to trail. Remove faded lower leaves. Clean plants with gentle spray of tepid water. Fertilize every 2 months, or apply at half recommended strength every month. Leach regularly to avoid damaging accumulation of soluble salts. Excess moisture can result in leaf, stem rots and leaf spots. Check for mealybugs, thrips, spider mites, and scale insects.

P. 'Black Cardinal': cluster of big deep purple leaves on short vine.
P. 'Emerald King': strong green spade-shaped leaves resist disease.
P. 'Emerald Queen': compact yet vigorous vine has deep green foliage with short stems; uniform leaf size.
P. 'Florida': five-lobed leaves on flexible stems; pinch tips for fuller, more bushy growth.
P. 'Pluto': compact, self-supporting cluster of deep purple-green lobed leaves; very tolerant.

Philodendron scandens subsp. oxycardium

Philodendron 'Red Princess'

Philodendron 'Red Emerald'

Philodendron selloum

Phoenix roebelenii

P. 'Red Emerald': 12-15" (30-38cm) heart- or spade-shaped leaves are glossy dark green with red undersides, veins, stems.

P. 'Red Princess': compact, vigorous vine; leaves coppery-red as they unfurl, mature deep green.

P. 'Royal Queen': reddish-green leaves on compact, self-supporting red stems.

P. 'Xanadu': self-supporting stems bear prolific lobed green leaves.

P. bipennifolium (by-pe-ni-FOH-li-um)
[*P. panduraeformae* (pan-dew-ri-FOR-mee)]
Fiddle-leaf Philodendron, Horsehead Philodendron, Panda Plant
Slow-growing, sturdy vine has shapely dark green leaves on long stems.

P. scandens subsp. *oxycardium* (SKAN-denz ok-si-KAR-di-um)
[*P. cordatum* (kor-DAH-tum)]
Heartleaf Philodendron, Parlor Ivy
Familiar heart-shaped green leaves on slender, flexible vines. Grows rapidly. New leaves may become larger as plant matures.

P. selloum (se-LOH-um)
[*P. bipinnatifidum* (by-pi-na-ti-FID-um)]
Tree Philodendron, Lacy Tree Philodendron
Self-supporting tree grows to height of 3-4' (0.9-1.2m), with equal or greater spread. Allow space for natural, uncrowded growth.

PHOENIX (FEE-niks)   WA - MS
Date Palm
Tropical and subtropical feather palms. Leafy rosettes when young; stout trunks with persistent leaf-bases later. Pleated leaflets on gracefully arching leafstems. Durable container plants. Prefer humid climate; tolerate dry air. Grow in well-draining, rich, humusy palm mix.
MAINTENANCE In winter, let soil become partly dry between waterings. Wipe leaves or wash with water to remove dust. Fertilize at half recommended strength every month spring through fall. Trim damaged and discolored foliage. Check for spider mites and scale insects.

P. canariensis (ka-ne-ree-EN-sis)   BL
Canary Island Date Palm
Massive, formal palm for large containers, malls. Prefers cooler indoor climate; outdoor specimens withstand cold, frost. Tolerates salt and desert climate. Grows slowly to about 60' (18m).

P. roebelenii (roh-be-LIN-ee-y)   ML
Miniature Date Palm, Pygmy Date Palm
Dwarf date palm has graceful rosette of dark green feathery leaves on bristly short trunk. Height 4-12' (1.2-3.6m). Easy to grow. Tolerates air-conditioning, short periods of low light. If possible, move to shaded outdoor position during warm months.

Pilea 'Moon Valley'

Pilea involucrata

Pilea cadieri

Pilea depressa

Pilea microphylla

PILEA (PY-lee-a)   ML - WA - PD

Tropical small foliage plants for warm indoor climates. Shrubby or trailing habit, attractive patterned foliage. Specimen or accent for table, desk; useful in dish gardens, as groundcover or filler for plant groups. Grow in general indoor mix; repot as needed. Propagate from stem cuttings.

MAINTENANCE Let soil dry more between waterings in winter. Pinch shoot tips to encourage branching. Trim off weak, leggy growth. Fertilize at half recommended strength every 3-6 weeks spring through fall, less often in winter. Leach regularly to avoid damaging accumulation of soluble salts. Best with relative humidity 30% or more. Overwatering, soggy soil, and drought result in leaf drop. Check for mealybugs, spider mites, whitefly.

P. 'Moon Valley'
Imperial Panamiga
Broad, deeply quilted leaves with bronzed centers.

P. cadieri (ka-dee-EH-ry, ka-dee-EH-ree-y)
Watermelon Plant, Aluminum Plant
Silvery markings on quilted leaves. Height 10-15" (25-38cm).

P. depressa (de-PRES-a) and
P. nummulariifolia (nu-mew-lah-ree-y-FOH-li-a)
Creeping Pilea, Baby Tears, Creeping Charlie
Branching spreaders with masses of tiny pea-green leaves that are spoon-shaped (*P. depressa*) or rounded (*P. nummulariifolia*) on trailing, often reddish stems. Good basket plant.

P. involucrata (in-vo-loo-KRAH-ta)
Friendship Plant, Panamiga
Coppery-brown markings intensify with brighter light. Quilted leaves are closely spaced, have wine purple undersides. Height 6-8" (15-20cm).

P. microphylla (my-kroh-FIL-a)
Artillery Plant
Soft clouds of feathery green leaves on upright succulent stems. Height to about 12" (30cm).

PITTOSPORUM (pi-TOS-poh-rum)   BL - CA - PD
P. tobira (toh-BEE-ra)
Japanese Pittosporum, Australian Laurel, Mock Orange
Evergreen shrub with tough, leathery leaves 2-4" (5-10cm) long. Height 2-6' (0.6-1.8m) indoors, 10-15' (3-4.5m) outdoors where hardy (zone 8). Orange blossom scented flowers in early summer. Tolerates par-

Platycerium bifurcatum

Pittosporum tobira

Platycerium hillii

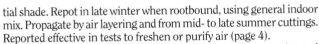
Pittosporum tobira 'Variegata'

tial shade. Repot in late winter when rootbound, using general indoor mix. Propagate by air layering and from mid- to late summer cuttings. Reported effective in tests to freshen or purify air (page 4).

'Variegata', **Variegated Mock Orange:** grayish green leaves variegated creamy-white. Best with moderate light. Slower growing than species.
MAINTENANCE Flowers indoors with sufficient light. Let soil dry more between waterings in winter when growth slows. Prune to shape in late winter before new growth develops. Clean with spray of tepid water. Fertilize at half recommended strength every 2-4 months spring through fall. Leach regularly to avoid damaging accumulation of soluble salts that cause foliar wilt, brown leaf margins. Excessive humidity results in leaf spots. Check for scale insects, aphids, mealybugs.

PLATYCERIUM (pla-ti-SEE-ri-um)   ML - CA - H - PD
Staghorn Fern, Elk's-horn Fern, Antelope-ears
Epiphytic ferns with big leathery fronds. Sterile fronds form water-storing shield over roots; fork-ended fertile fronds arch out from center of shield. Specimen to hang on wood, wire support; in basket or shallow container; or reduce soil depth with deep under-layer of broken clean pot. Slow growing. Mount to hang, with sphagnum moss under shield. Plant in containers with osmunda fibers or humus-rich fern mix. Propagate from suckers that form at base.

MAINTENANCE Soak hanging fern's rootball in room temperature water when root area is dry — once or twice each week. Protect from drafts. Spray gently with tepid water to clean. Fertilize at one-quarter recommended strength every 4-6 weeks while growing; use only liquid fertilizer. Leaf edges will scorch in dry air, drafts.

P. bifurcatum (by-fur-KAH-tum)
[*P. alcicorne* (al-chi-KOR-nee)]
Common Staghorn Fern, Elk's-horn Fern
Apple green, branching fertile fronds arch and droop to 36" (90cm).
'Netherlands', Regina Wilhelmina Staghorn Fern: shorter, broader, gray-green fertile fronds arch in all directions from central pale green shield. Tolerates drier air than many ferns.

P. hillii (HIL-ee-y)
Elk's-horn Fern
Blue-green fronds have very broad antler-like tips.

HUMIDITY (page 7)
   H - Best with relative humidity 50% or more.

Plectranthus australis

Plectranthus oertendahlii

Plectranthus australis 'Variegatus'

Plectranthus madagascariensis 'Variegated Mintleaf'

PLECTRANTHUS (plek-TRAN-thus)   ML - CA - PD
Swedish Begonia, Swedish Ivy, Prostrate Coleus

Fast-growing spreading and trailing foliage plant has upright spikes of flowers with sufficient light. Easy to grow, quickly fills container. Specimen basket plant, ground cover for plant groups. Rapid growth. Replace older plants with rooted cuttings, several in container with well-draining general indoor mix. Propagate from cuttings.

MAINTENANCE Tolerates minimum night temperatures down to 50°F (10°C). Water less often when growth is slow. Pinch stem tips to encourage branching. Prune out leggy, overgrown stems. Fertilize at half recommended strength every 1-2 months, more when growth is rapid and less when growth slows. Leach regularly to avoid damaging accumulation of soluble salts. Root rots result from overwatering. Check for mealybugs and whitefly.

P. australis (aw-STRAH-lis)
[*P. nummularius, P. verticillatus*]
Swedish Ivy, Creeping Charlie
Dark green, waxy leaves on fleshy spreading stems. Small white flowers cluster on erect stems.
'Variegatus' (ve-ri-e-GAH-tus), **Variegated Swedish Ivy:** Creamy white, irregular variegations.

P. coleoides 'Variegatus' (ko-lee-OI-deez ve-ri-e-GAH-tus)
[*P. c.* 'Marginatus' (mar-ji-NAH-tus), *P. forsteri* (FOR ste-ry)]
Candle Plant, White-edged Swedish Ivy
Vigorous trailing plant mounds 8-12" (20-30cm) without support. Clusters of white-purple flowers.

P. madagascariensis 'Variegated Mintleaf'
Mounding, trailing plant has fragrant foliage with irregular white and green variegations.

P. oertendahlii (ur-ten-DAH-lee-y)
Prostrate Coleus, Spurflower, Velvet Swedish Ivy
Rounded, dark green leaves with white veins, reddish undersides.

PODOCARPUS (poh-doh-KAR-pus)   BL - CA - MS
Evergreen conifer with slender needles on upright, spreading, and drooping branches. Shrub or small tree grows 3-6' (0.9-1.8m) indoors. Specimen for tub, interiorscape planter. Tolerates cool drafts, though new growth may be damaged. Repot rarely. Grow in well-draining, slightly acid indoor mix with added sand and peat moss. Propagate from seed and fall stem cuttings.

MAINTENANCE Let soil surface dry between waterings in winter. Root rots result from overwatering or poor drainage. Prune to shape in spring. Fertilize every 3-6 months. Check for scale insects.

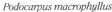

Podocarpus macrophyllus   *Podocarpus macrophyllus* 'Maki'   *Polypodium punctatum* 'Grandiceps'

Polypodium polypodioides

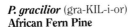

Polypodium aureum

P. gracilior (gra-KIL-i-or)
African Fern Pine
Habit varies from small dish garden plant to trailing vine to woody shrub. Soft, bluish-green needles, 1-2" (2.5-5cm) long.

P. macrophyllus (mak-roh-FIL-us)
Southern Yew, Buddhist Pine
Strong green 2-4" (5-10cm) needles have paler undersides.
'Maki' (MAY-ky): shrub has shorter needles, more densely packed on upright branches.

POLYPODIUM (po-li-POH-di-um)   ML - WA - PD
Polypody Ferns
Epiphytic ferns adapt well to soil and airy indoor conditions. Woolly rhizomes extend across soil surface, over edge of container. Long, arched fronds. Spreading specimen or accent plants for table, pedestal, basket. Tolerate nights as cool as 50°F (10°C), and dry soil for short periods. Sparse fibrous roots. Grow in shallow container like half-pot or azalea pot, or reduce soil depth with deep under-layer of broken clean pot. Plant on well-draining humusy indoor or basic fern mix; repot infrequently. Propagate by division.
MAINTENANCE Benefits from moderate sunlight in colder weather. In winter, let soil dry more between waterings. Protect from drafts.

Clean with spray of tepid water. Fertilize at one-quarter recommended strength every 4-6 weeks while growing. Best with relative humidity 30% or more. Leaflet edges will burn in dry air, drafts.

P. aureum (AW-ree-um)
[*Phlebodium aureum* (fle-BPOH-dee-um)]
Rabbit's-foot Fern, Hare's-foot Fern, Golden Polypody
Deeply cut blue-green leaves grow 36" (90cm) long, 10" (25cm) wide. Golden spores mass under fertile leaflets. Orange-brown rhizomes.
P. a. var. aereolatum (a-ree-oh-LAH-tum): easily grown variety with broader leaf segments and rusty brown rhizomes..
'Mayi' ['Undulatum']: arching fronds have undulating edges.

P. polypodioides (po-li-poh-dee-OI-deez)
Resurrection Fern
Small species that becomes dormant when rhizomes dry out. Tolerates frost. Grows on tree bark or log, and on moist acid, humusy soil.

P. punctatum 'Grandiceps' (punk-TAH-tum GRAN-di-cheps)
[*Microsorium punctatum* cv. (mik-roh-SOR-i-um)]
Climbing Bird's-nest Fern
Slow-growing, with yellow-green, upright, forked and crested fronds.

Polyscias balfouriana

Polyscias fruticosa

Polyscias balfouriana 'Marginata'

Polyscias guilfoylei

POLYSCIAS (po-LIS-i-as) ML/BL - WA - PD

Tropical evergreen shrubs and small trees for warm, humid locations. Gracefully curving green stems mature light gray-brown. Single or multiple trunk specimens grow indoors to 4-8' (1.2-2.4m). Divided leaves have variable leaflets. Small plants useful in larger dish gardens; larger accents for tubs, plant groups, interiorscapes. Slow growth. Grow in general indoor mix; repot infrequently. Propagate from stem tip or stem section cuttings, or by air layering.

MAINTENANCE Avoid direct scorching sun. Let soil dry more between waterings in winter. Prune to shape. Clean with gentle spray of tepid water. Fertilize at half recommended strength every 3-4 months to match healthy new growth. Leach regularly to avoid damaging accumulation of soluble salts. Best with relative humidity 30% or more. Leaves may be lost after move to drier location; new foliage will develop. Protect from drafts, air pollution. Check for spider mites, scale insects, mealybugs.

P. balfouriana (bal-for-ree-AH-na)
[*P. scutellaria* 'Balfourii' (skew-te-LAY ri-a)]
Dinner Plate Aralia, Balfour Aralia
Gleaming bright green, rounded leaflets on upright stems.
'Marginata': white-edged foliage.

P. fruticosa (froo-ti-KOH-sa)
Ming Aralia
Graceful, lacy and fern-like leaves on light willowy stems. Height 6-8' (1.8-2.4m).
'Elegans' (EL-e-ganz): compact form, dark green foliage.

P. guilfoylei (gil-FOY-lee-y)
Geranium-leaf Aralia, Wild Coffee
Leaflets big ovals or may be finely cut. Dark green foliage often has white edges or splashes.
'Blackie', Black Aralia: puckered, deeply quilted leaves are dark black-green. Easy to grow.

LIGHT for indoor plants (page 6)
LL - LOW LIGHT: performs well in low light conditions, or shade.
ML - MODERATE LIGHT: performs well in part shade or diffused light.
BL - BRIGHT LIGHT: performs well in full sun or bright indirect light.

WATERING (page 8)
MS - Keep soil moist.
PD - Let soil become partly dry between waterings.
DS - Allow soil to dry out between thorough waterings.

Polystichum tsus-simense

Polystichum setosum

Poterium saguisorba: burnet

POLYSTICHUM (po-LIS-ti-kum)   **ML/LL - CA - H - PD**
Shield Fern
Small to medium size deep green ferns with distinctly triangular divided fronds. Dish garden, terrarium plant; accents for table, basket. Grow outdoors in mild climates. Tolerate dry soil for short periods. Grow in humusy indoor or basic fern mix. Propagate by division.
MAINTENANCE Adapt to warmth of terrarium; also tolerate nights as cool as 32°F (0°C). Spray with plain water to clean foliage; avoid chemicals. Fertilize at one-quarter recommended strength every 4-6 weeks, or with weaker solution at every watering while growth is active. Roots can be damaged by stronger applications. As growth slows reduce watering, stop fertilizing, and set plant in cooler area. Leach regularly to avoid damaging accumulation of soluble salts. Cut off old and discolored fronds. Check for slugs and snails on plants moved in from shade outdoors, and for scale insects, spider mites, and mealybugs.

P. setosum (se-TOH-sum)
Bristle Fern
Low, spreading fronds have bristly tips and brown, hairy stems. Best in higher humidity environments, tolerates low light.

P. tsus-simense (TSOO-si-MEN-see)
Dwarf Leather Fern
Compact fern grows about 12" (30cm) tall, spreads 8-12" (20-30cm).

POTERIUM (poh-TEH-ee-um)   **BL - CA - PD**
P. sanguisorba (san-gwi-SOR-ba)
[*Sanguisorba minor* (MY-nor)]
Burnet, Garden Burnet, Salad Burnet
Fast-growing perennial herb best grown from seed each year for continued supply of young leaves. Compound, lacy foliage in basal rosette; flowering stems rise to 24" (60cm). Add fresh leaves for light cucumber flavor in salads, cold drinks. Dry leaves for crumbling into soups, salad dressing. Long taproot. Easily grown from seed sown onto general indoor mix in deep container. Also propagated by division.
MAINTENANCE Harvest leaves regularly and cut plant back to 4-5" (10-13cm) to remove flower stems and encourage fresh leafy growth. Fertilize at half recommended strength every 2-4 weeks when growth is vigorous; every 4-8 weeks during winter.

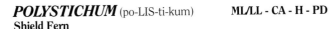

TEMPERATURE (page 7)
  CA - COOL to AVERAGE TEMPERATURES: days 60-75°F (16-24°C), nights as cool as 45°F (7°C).
  WA - AVERAGE to WARM TEMPERATURES: days 70-80°F (21-27°C), nights 60-65°F (16-18°C).

| *Primula* ✕*polyantha* | *Primula* ✕*polyantha* | *Primula* ✕*polyantha* |

| *Primula* ✕*polyantha* | *Primula malacoides* | *Primula malacoides* |

PRIMULA (PRIM-ew-la)　　　　　ML - CA - H - PD

Colorful flowering plants for cool, bright indoor locations. Several types with more or less dainty blossom clusters, rounded or long quilted leaves. Use individually or massed for seasonal displays. Grow in well-draining humusy indoor mix. Indoor primulas are short-lived perennials grown from seed, discarded after flowering. *P.* ✕*polyantha* will grow outdoors in zones 3-8; propagate by division and from seed.
MAINTENANCE Grow in cool, bright, humid place. Water to keep soil evenly moist until flowers develop. Then let soil surface become dry between waterings. Fertilize at half recommended strength every 3-6 weeks before flowering. Check for leaf spot disease, spider mites, and whitefly.

P. malacoides (ma-la-KOI-deez)
Baby Primrose, Fairy Primrose
Lacy clusters of delicately colored flowers on slender stems, 8-16" (20-40cm) above soft, rounded, fresh green foliage. Short-lived perennial treated as annual.
AFTER FLOWERING, water less often as plant dies.

P. ✕*polyantha* (po-lee-AN-tha)
Polyanthus, Polyantha Primrose, Lady's Fingers
Primrose-like plants with long leaves below blossom clusters. Many vibrant colors.
AFTER FLOWERING, continue to water and resume regular fertilizer applications while growth continues. May be moved to sheltered location outside during summer; for indoor flowering, bring back inside before frost. Maintain dormant perennial primroses through winter in cool, bright room, keeping soil barely moist. As growth restarts, water more frequently; resume fertilizer applications when first leaves are fully expanded.

SUPPLEMENTARY LIGHT
Although plants may not make new growth in low light (fewer than 100 foot candles) they can remain attractive for long periods. In addition, and especially for interior landscapes, office and reception areas, rapid plant growth may be neither needed nor desired. Combine several sources of light (artificial and natural) for sufficient light to sustain plants.

Pteris cretica 'Albo-lineata'

Pteris cretica 'Wilsonii'

Pteris cretica 'Wimsettii'

Pteris multifida

Pteris ensiformis 'Victoriae'

Pteris quadriaurita 'Argyraea'

PTERIS (TER-is)   ML/BL - WA - PD
Brake, Dish Fern, Table Fern

Small tropical ferns adapted to indoor climates. Fronds divided into relatively few, often ribbon-like leaflets. Use in terrariums and dish gardens; specimen or accent for small tables; group plantings, interiorscapes. Slow growing. Grow in pots or baskets in general or humusy indoor mix, or in basic fern mix. Propagate by division.

MAINTENANCE Good in unbroken north light or filtered east light. Benefits from moderate sunlight during colder weather. Water to keep soil lightly moist; do not let plants wilt. Spray with plain water to clean foliage; avoid chemicals. Fertilize at one-quarter recommended strength every 4-6 weeks, or with weaker solution at every watering while growth is active. Delicate roots can be damaged by stronger applications. Best with relative humidity 30% or more; tolerates drier air than many ferns. Cut off old and discolored fronds. Leaflet edges will scorch in extra-dry air, drafts. Check for slugs and snails on plants moved in from shade outdoors, and for scale insects, mealybugs, and whitefly.

P. cretica cultivars (KREH-ti-ka)

Many named cultivars, most have upright to spreading fronds. Height and spread 10-18" (25-45cm).

'**Albo-lineata**' (AL-bo-li-nee-AH-ta), **Variegated Table Fern:** broad creamy-white central band on each leaflet.

'**Mayii**' (MAY-ee-y): smaller version of 'Albo-lineata' with crested tips.
'**Parkeri**': finely toothed, green leaflets.
'**Roweii**' (ROH-ee-y), **Crested Brake:** frilled and crested green leaflets.
'**Wilsonii**', **Fan Table Fern:** bright green crested fronds.
'**Wimsettii**' (wim-SET-ee-y), **Skeleton Table Fern:** dainty fronds with tasseled and forked tips.

P. ensiformis cultivars (en-si-FOR-mis)
Sword Brake

Upright fronds with smaller leaflets.
'**Evergemiensis**' (e-ver-je-mi-EN-sis): silvery-white central band, dark green margins.
'**Victoriae**', **Victoria Fern, Silver Leaf Fern:** silvery markings on leaflets.

P. multifida (mul-ti-FID-a)
Chinese Brake

Slender, ribbon-like leaflets have crested tips.

P. quadriaurita '**Argyraea**' (kwod-ri-aw-REE-ta)   LL - CA - H
Silver Fern, Silver-lace Fern

Blue-green leaves grow to 36" (90cm) long and half as wide. Leaflets marked with silver centers. Tolerates lower light, needs higher humidity than other table ferns.

Rhipsalidopsis gaertneri

Rhipsalidopsis rosea

Rhapis excelsa

RHAPIS (RAY-pis)   ML - WA - MS
Lady Palm
Slow-growing palm grows in clump with bamboo-like stems and dark green foliage. Graceful, upright fronds topped with fan of notch-tipped leaflets. Tolerate short periods of shade, and nights as cool as 50°F (10°C). Prefers humid climate though tolerates dry air. Grow in well-draining, rich, humusy palm mix. Propagate by division; let soil dry between waterings until divisions are well-rooted.
MAINTENANCE In winter, let soil become partly dry between waterings. Wipe leaves or wash with water to remove dust. Fertilize every month spring through fall. Trim damaged and discolored foliage. Check for spider mites, mealybugs, and scale insects.

R. excelsa (ek-SEL-sa)
Bamboo Palm, Slender Lady Palm, Miniature Fan Palm, Fern Rhapis
Durable indoor palm, grows to about 5' (1.5m) indoors, with 6-12" (15-30cm) fans. Fine container palm. Several cultivars, including **'Variegata'** (ve-ri-e-GAH-ta), **Variegated Lady Palm**, which has green and ivory striped leaflets.

R. humilis (HEW-mi-lis)
Reed Rhapis
Very slow-growing, reed-like stems. Height 9-18' (2.7-5.4m).

RHIPSALIDOPSIS (rip-sa-li-DOP-sis)   ML - WA /CA - PD
Flowering epiphytic cacti with branched, jointed, arching stems. Tolerate drought. Good basket plants. Grow in well-draining humusy indoor mix; repot infrequently. Propagate from stem cuttings that include several joints.

R. gaertneri cultivars (GART-ne-ry)
[*Hatiora gaertneri* (ha-tee-OR-a)]
Easter Cactus
Smooth, rounded, spine-free stem sections. Named cultivars have orange, red, or pink flowers.

R. rosea (RHO-see-a)
[*Hatiora rosea*]
Rose Easter Cactus
Smaller, denser plant has 3-5 angled jointed stems with red-tinged edges and short bristles. Scented, rose-pink flowers.

AFTER FLOWERING, plants rest before making new growth; let soil dry between waterings. When new growth starts, water to keep soil slightly moist. Fertilize at half recommended strength every 2-4 weeks, early spring through summer; none in fall and winter. After mid-summer, reduce water and fertilizer applications. Flower buds form when plant rests with shorter days, drier soil, and cooler nights.
MAINTENANCE Provide warm temperatures while growing and cool

Rhododendron

Rhododendron

Rhododendron

Rhoeo spathacea

when dormant, usually in winter. Let soil remain dry for longer periods between waterings in fall and winter. Clean with gentle spray of water. Needs relative humidity of 30% or more. Constantly moist soil or poor drainage causes yellow stems and root losses. Check for mealybugs, scale insects, and aphids.

RHODODENDRON (roh-do-DEN-dron)   BL - CA - MS/PD
Azalea
Flowering shrubs for seasonal display, foliage interest. Blossoms last 1-2 months in cool, humid indoor location. Grow in well-draining, acid, humusy indoor mix; repot infrequently. Propagate from shoot or stem cuttings.
Reported effective in tests to freshen or purify air (page 4).
AFTER FLOWERING, prune off spent blossoms. Continue regular waterings. After spring frost, give sheltered position outdoors. Apply acid fertilizer at half recommended strength every 2-4 weeks spring and summer. Trim new growth to shape until midsummer. Flower buds form in late summer and fall. As nights get cooler, reduce watering frequency and fertilize every 4-6 weeks. Bring azalea in before frost. Keep in cool, bright room for 1-2 months before flower color shows.
MAINTENANCE Avoid direct scorching sun. Keep soil moist but not soggy while flowers are open. No fertilizer needed while flowering. Best with relative humidity 30% or more. Protect from drafts. Check for spider mites, scale insects.

RHOEO (REE-oh)   ML - CA - PD
R. spathacea (spa-THAH-see-a)
[*R. discolor, Tradescantia spathacea*]
Moses-in-the-cradle, Oyster Plant, Boat Lily, Purple-leaved Spiderwort
Stiff-leaved foliage plant with thick, flexible stems that rise 8-12" (20-30cm), then spread and trail. Tiny white flowers nestle between boat-like bracts at leaf bases. Dark green leaves have purple undersides. Variegated forms offer striped foliage. Good basket plant. Slender roots. Grow in well-draining general indoor mix; repot infrequently. Propagate by division and from stem cuttings.
MAINTENANCE Clean with gentle spray of tepid water. Fertilize at half recommended strength every 3-4 months. Leach regularly to avoid damaging accumulation of soluble slats. Leaf losses result from excessively wet or dry soil; plant dies back with high salts. Check for stem rot, leaf spot diseases, mealybugs, and spider mites.

TO LEACH PLANTS — Water well four or five times in succession, discarding all drainage water. For a more thorough leaching, saturate the soil by immersing the whole container almost to its brim; leave to soak for 10-15 minutes; remove, and allow soil to drain. Repeat several times.

Miniature Rose

Miniature Rose

Miniature Rose

Miniature Rose

Rosmarinus officinalis: rosemary

ROSA (RHO-za)   BL - CA - PD

Small seasonal flowering plants for bright indoor positions. Variously colored blossoms on truly miniature bushes. Plant in general indoor mix; repot as needed to renew soil. Propagate from stem cuttings.

AFTER FLOWERING, continue to water and fertilize regularly while plant is growing. Move outdoors to sheltered place, full sun in temperate zones. Prune and repot in fall. In winter, plants may rest outdoors or in cool indoor room, or continue to grow in cool, bright location. Keep soil barely moist when resting; or water sparingly to maintain active foliage and developing flower buds.

MAINTENANCE Wash regularly with spray of water to clean foliage and discourage spider mites. Fertilize every 3-6 weeks while growing rapidly, usually spring and summer. Best with relative humidity 30% or more. Trim faded flowers, yellowed leaves. Poor light results in leaf losses, non-flowering. Check for powdery mildew, aphids, spider mites.

ROSMARINUS (rohz-ma-REE-nus)   BL/ML - CA - MS/PD
Rosemary
R. officinalis cultivars (o-fi-si-NAH-lis)

Small, shrubby, tender perennial herb grows well indoors. Several cultivars, height can vary 8-24" (20-60cm). Use fragrant, blue-green needle-like leaves fresh or dry with meat, poultry, and vegetables, and in soups, stuffing or dressing, and sauces. Violet-blue or white flowers. Grow in well-draining general indoor mix with added limestone to reduce acidity. Propagate from stem cuttings.

MAINTENANCE Keep soil slightly moist, especially when plant is young. Fertilize at half recommended strength every 2-4 weeks when growth is vigorous; every 4-8 weeks during winter.

RUMOHRA (roo-MOH-ra)   ML - CA - MS/PD
R. adiantiformis (a-dee-an-ti-FOR-mis)
Leather Fern, Leatherleaf Fern, Iron Fern

Sturdy, durable, bushy fern for indoor climates. Dark green, leathery leaves on stiff stems, long-lasting, used by florists in fresh arrangements. Tolerates some hot sun, also cold temperatures (light frost outdoors). Fast to moderate growth. Fibrous roots. Grow in humusy indoor or basic fern mix. Propagate by division.

MAINTENANCE Benefits from sunlight during colder weather. Water to keep soil lightly moist; in winter, let soil become partly dry between waterings. Avoid chemical sprays. Fertilize at one-quarter recommended strength every 4-6 weeks, or with weaker solution at every watering while growth is active. Best with relative humidity 30% or more; tolerates drier air than many ferns. Leaflet edges scorch in extra-dry air, drafts. Check for slugs and snails on plants moved in from shade outdoors, and for scale insects, mealybugs, and spider mites.

Rumohra adiantiformis

Saintpaulia Optimara hybrid 'Virginia'

Saintpaulia 'Crafty Farmer'

Saintpaulia Ballet hybrid 'Linda'

Saintpaulia Ballet hybrid 'Sabrina'

Miniature *Saintpaulia* 'Icicle Trinket'

SAINTPAULIA (saynt-PAW-li-a)   ML/BL - WA - PD
African Violet

Colorful flowering gesneriads have rosettes of oval or rounded velvety leaves with clusters of showy blossoms. Easy to grow, needing less humidy than other gesneriads. Shallow, fibrous roots. Grow in humusy gesneriad mix. Repot only as needed to renew crowded or overgrown plants. Propagate by division, from leaf cuttings and seed.

AFTER FLOWERING, plants rest briefly then reflower with adequate light. Trim off dead flowers. While not in flower, use general indoor plant fertilizer at half recommended strength every 3-6 weeks.

MAINTENANCE Best with sun in winter, diffused bright light in summer. Water when soil surface is dry. Apply high phosphate fertilizer at half recommended strength every 3-6 weeks while in flower. Leach regularly to avoid salts damage to sensitive roots. Tolerates normal home humidity yet grows and flowers more readily with relative humidity 30% or more. Remove all dead and damaged parts to eliminate potential infection sites. Irregular and excessive watering can result in crown rot. Misshapen and streaked foliage indicates virus: discard plant. Check for botrytis blight, mealybugs, aphids, spider mites.

Miniature African Violets: truly miniature forms rarely exceed the confines of 2½ or 3 inch (6 or 8cm) containers. Rosette or semi-trailing plants for windowsills, terrariums. Best with relative humidity 30% or more.

Trailing African Violets: informal, rapidly spreading plants develop many rosettes. Flowering almost continuous with sufficient light. Good in hanging baskets.

S. ionantha cultivars and hybrids (y-oh-NAN-tha)
African Violet

Leafy rosettes spread 6-10" (15-25cm). Colorful flower clusters rise above and among foliage. Many varieties originated from this and other species; several named groups:

Ballet African Violets: wide range of color, form. Striking clear colors. Flowers often double and ruffled. Tolerate adverse home conditions.

Optimara African Violets: clusters of big, long-lasting flowers on formal leafy rosettes. Some have wavy or frilled petal edges. Vivid colors.

Rhapsodie African Violets: abundant and long-lasting blossoms. Easily grown. Faded flowers do not drop so must be trimmed by hand. Remove some leaves to help flower buds push through dense leafy rosettes.

S. intermedia (in-ter-MEE-di-a)

Informal rosettes of faintly toothed, long-stemmed leaves. Delicate violet-colored blossoms in loose clusters.

Salvia officinalis: sage

Sansevieria trifasciata 'Moonglow'

Sansevieria trifasciata 'Hahnii'

Sansevieria trifasciata 'Golden Hahnii'

Sansevieria trifasciata 'Laurentii'

SALVIA (SAL-vi-a)   BL - CA - PD
Sage
S. officinalis (o-fi-si-NAH-lis)

Shrubby perennial herb with 2" (5cm) gray-green leaves. Some forms have variegated foliage, darker purple flowers. Combine chopped fresh or powdered dry leaves with thyme and marjoram to flavor stuffing or dressing, sausage, soup, cheese dishes, and tea. Grow in general indoor mix with added limestone to reduce acidity. Propagate from seed, cuttings, divisions.

MAINTENANCE Trim regularly to contain height and encourage fresh new growth. Fertilize at half recommended strength every 2-4 weeks when growth is vigorous; every 4-8 weeks during winter.

SANSEVIERIA (san-se-vi-EH-ri-a)   LL/ML - WA - DS
S. trifasciata (try-ta-see-AH-ta)
Snake Plant, Mother-in-Law's Tongue

Durable succulent foliage plant with tall, upright clusters of stiff leaves. Broad crossbands of grayish-green decorate dark green foliage. Height 3-4' (0.9-1.2m). Easy to grow, tolerates neglect and wide range of temperatures. Specimen or accent for table or shelf; leaf shape contrast in group planting; mass for larger scale accent. Small rosette forms

for dish gardens, massed for ground cover. Rhizomes have short, thick roots. Plant in short containers with sandy indoor mix; divide and repot every few years to prevent overcrowding. Propagate by division or from leaf sections. Cultivars offer different color variations and short, spreading rosettes best viewed from above.

Reported effective in tests to freshen or purify air (page 4).

'Hahnii' (HAH-nee-y), **Birds-nest Sansevieria:** short, spreading rosettes in dark green with grayish markings. Height about 4" (10cm), spread 6-8" (15-20cm).

'Golden Hahnii', **Golden Birds-nest Sansevieria:** creamy yellow striping on short fleshy leaves.

'Laurentii' (lo-REN-tee-y), [*S. t.* var. *laurentii*], **Snake Plant:** tall clustered leaves have yellow margins. Leaf sections yield all-green new plants: propagate by division for yellow variegation.

'Moonglow' ['Moonshine', 'Silver Moon']: clustered leaves are creamy silver-green.

MAINTENANCE Let soil remain dry for longer periods between waterings in winter. Constantly moist soil or poor drainage causes yellow leaves and loss of roots. Clean with moist soft cloth or gentle spray of water. Fertilize at half recommended strength every 2-3 months spring through fall.

Sansevieria trifasciata

Satureja hortensis: summer savory

Sarracenia purpurea

Satureja montana: winter savory

SARRACENIA (sa-ra-SEE-nee-a)　　BL - CA - H - MS
Pitcher Plant

Insectivorous plant, native to eastern North America. Several species: upright or prostrate pitchers with size range 4-36" (10-90cm). Pitcher structure and secretions attract and trap insects. Colorful, long-lasting flowers open spring to summer. Thick, strap-like winter leaves. Grow in full pots or terrarium, with very acid mix (pH 4.0-4.5) containing equal volumes of peat moss and washed sharp sand. Propagate from rhizome cuttings or seed.

MAINTENANCE Avoid direct scorching sun. Provide shade when temperature exceeds 90°F (32°C). Best winter minimum temperature is 32°F (0°C); long periods above 60°F (15°C) break dormancy, resulting in weaker growth next season. Water with distilled or soft rainwater to avoid damaging lime contamination. Maintain moist soil spring through fall by setting container in 1/2-1" (1.5-2.5cm) soft lime-free or distilled water. Let soil become partly dry during winter dormancy. Carefully clip out old, discolored leaves. Do not fertilize, especially if pitcher plant can be moved to semi-shaded outdoor area in warm weather. Pitchers do not develop correctly if plant is well-nourished. Added chemicals may also damage sensitive plant tissues.

SATUREJA (sa-tew-REE-ya)　　BL - CA - PD
Savory, Calamint

Low-growing herbs with narrow foliage and profuse pinkish or white flowers. Use leaves in stuffings or dressings, salads, soups, and sauces, and in meat, fish, poultry and egg dishes. Grow in general indoor mix with added limestone to reduce acidity. Propagate from seed, or by division and cuttings.

MAINTENANCE Trim regularly to contain height and spread. Fertilize at half recommended strength every 2-4 weeks when growth is vigorous; every 4-8 weeks during winter.

S. hortensis (hor-TEN-sis)
Summer Savory

Lightly flavored annual grows rapidly from direct-sown seeds.

S. montana (mon-TAH-na)
Winter Savory

Perennial species has stronger flavor. Use more sparingly than summer savory.

Saxifraga stolonifera

Schefflera (Brassaia) actinophylla

SAXIFRAGA (sak-SIF-ra-ga)   ML - CA - PD/DS
S. stolonifera (stoh-lo-NIF-e-ra)
[*S. sarmentosa* (sar-men-TOH-sa)]

Mother-of-thousands, Strawberry Begonia, Strawberry Geranium
Spreading rosettes of rounded, silver-veined, deep green leaves with purplish undersides. Informal plant spreads like strawberry, with plantlets on runners. Erect stems bear clusters of dainty white blossoms in summer. Useful small specimen for table or hanging basket; ground cover in group planting. Hardy outdoors with protection and shade. Small root system. Grow in well-draining general indoor mix; repot each year. Propagate by division and from plantlets.
'Tricolor', Magic-carpet: dark green leaves variegated gray-green and ivory with pinkish flush.
MAINTENANCE Keep soil moist only during times of vigorous growth; allow at least some drying when growth slows. Overwatering can result in root rots. Fertilize every 3-4 months. Leach regularly to avoid damaging accumulation of soluble salts. Protect from drafts. Check for spider mites, whitefly, mealybugs.

SCHEFFLERA (shef-LEE-ra)   ML/BL - WA - PD
Umbrella Tree, Starleaf
Tropical foliage shrubs and small trees make handsome, durable foliage plants. Leaves palmately divided, umbrella-like. Widths vary; allow space for natural spread. Single or multiple stem specimens for low table, floor. Easy to grow. Move outdoors in summer, or plant in sheltered location in warmer climates. Tolerate cooler nights, down to 45°F (7°C). Fast-growing. Grow in general indoor mix; repot as needed. Propagate by air-layering or from mainstem cuttings.
MAINTENANCE In winter, let soil dry more between waterings. Avoid direct scorching sun. Cut back longest stem(s) or reduce height to contain size. Wipe leaves with moist cloth to remove dust. Mist or wash to discourage spider mites. Fertilize at half recommended strength every 4-8 weeks. Good air circulation ensures rapid drying of foliage, avoids rots in humid conditions. Lower leaves drop with insufficient light. Leaf yellowing and burn results from cold drafts, sunscorch. Check for spider mites and scale insects.

S. actinophylla (ak-ti-noh-FIL-a)
[*Brassaia actinophylla* (bra-SAY-a)] (Also page 41)
Schefflera, Australian or **Queensland Umbrella Tree, Octopus Tree, Starleaf**
Evergreen tree, height 6-12' (1.8-3.6m) or more in containers. Glossy

Schefflera arboricola

Schlumbergera

Schefflera arboricola 'Jacqueline'

Schlumbergera

green leaflets 4-12" (10-30cm) long. Leaflet size increases with height. Thin, spindly growth in low light.

S. arboricola (ar-bo-RIK-oh-la)
[*Heptapleurum arboricolum* (hep-ta-PLER-um ar-bo-RIK-oh-lum)]
Hawaiian Elf Schefflera
Darker, denser schefflera with rounded, 2-4" (5-10cm) leaflets. Compact shrub. Best with relative humidity 30% or more.
'Gold Capella': light gold and pale green mottling on some leaflets in each group; borders and plain leaflets dark green.
'Jacqueline': leaflets irregularly marked with ivory-white.
Additional cultivars: **'Renate', 'Trinette'.**

SCHLUMBERGERA (shlum-BER-ge-ra) ML - WA/CA - PD
[*Zygocactus* (zy-goh-KAK-tus)]
Flowering epiphytic cacti with branched, arching and trailing stems. Many named cultivars with white, pink, red, and orange flowers that open from fall to spring. Stem sections have toothed edges. Easily grown flowering accents for basket, pedestal, table. Tolerate drought. Fibrous roots. Grow in well-draining humusy indoor mix; repot infrequently. Propagate from stem cuttings with 3-5 joints.
AFTER FLOWERING, plants rest before making new growth; let soil dry between waterings. When new growth starts, water to keep soil slightly moist. Fertilize at half recommended strength every 2-4 weeks from early spring to midsummer; none in fall and winter. After midsummer, reduce water and fertilizer applications. Flower buds form when plant rests after growing period, with shorter days, drier soil, and cooler nights.
MAINTENANCE Provide warm temperatures while growing and cool when dormant, usually in fall or winter. Let soil remain dry for longer periods between waterings during dormancy. Clean with gentle spray of water. Provide relative humidity of 30% or more. Constantly moist soil or poor drainage causes yellow stems and root losses. Check for mealybugs, scale insects, and aphids.

S. bridgesii cultivars (bri-JEZ-ee-y)
[*S. ×buckleyi*]
Christmas Cactus
Branching stems arch to about 12" (30cm) long. Stem joints have scalloped edges. Many cultivars.

S. truncata cultivars (trun-KAH-ta)
Thanksgiving Cactus, Crab Cactus, Claw Cactus, Yoke Cactus, Linkleaf
Fall-flowering cacti with distinctive serrations on margins.

Sedum morganianum

Sedum divergens

Scindapsus pictus 'Argyraeus'

Sedum rubrotinctum

Sedum sarmentosum 'Green Carpet'

SCINDAPSUS (skin-DAP-sus)   ML - WA - H - MS/PD

S. pictus 'Argyraeus' (PIK-tus ar-gy-REE-us)
[*Epipremnum pictum* 'Argyraeus' (e-pi-PREM-num PIK-tum)]
Satin Pothos
Tropical aroid for warm and humid yet airy conditions, baskets. Silver-spotted, deep green foliage; trailing, climbing stems easily develop aerial roots. Heart-shaped leaves about 3" (7.5cm) long. Leaf size increases as plants mature. Tolerates some shade. Grow in humusy indoor mix; repot infrequently. Propagate from stem cuttings.
MAINTENANCE Let soil dry more between waterings when growth slows in winter. Pinch stem tips to encourage branching; trim long, straggly stems. Remove faded or yellowing leaves. Fertilize every 3 months, or apply at half recommended strength every 4-6 weeks. Leach regularly to avoid damaging accumulation of soluble salts. Excess water results in leaf spots, rots. Check for scale insects, mealybugs.

SEDUM (SEE-dum)   BL - WA/CA - DS

Stonecrop, Orpine
Spreading and trailing or low shrubby succulents have narrow, fleshy leaves packed densely on branching stems. Good basket plant. Rarely flowers indoors. Grow outdoors in warmer climates. Tolerate low light conditions, cool temperatures. Grow in well-draining sandy indoor mix; repot infrequently. Propagate from leaf cuttings or by division.
MAINTENANCE Provide warm temperatures while growing and cool when dormant in winter. Let soil remain dry for longer periods between waterings during dormancy, though do not let leaves shrivel. Constantly moist soil or poor drainage causes leaf drop and root losses. Keep leaves dry to avoid rots. Fertilize at half recommended strength every month in spring and summer; none in winter.

S. divergens (dy-VER-jenz)
Old Man's Bones
Blunt leaves are thickly set on reddish creeping stems. Mounds 4-6" (10-15cm).

S. morganianum (mor-ga-nee-AH-num)
Burro's-tail, Donkey's-tail
Slow growing basket plant has gray-green leaves on trailing stems that hang as long as 3' (90cm). Place away from traffic to avoid damage; leaves drop at slightest touch.

S. rubrotinctum (roo-broh-TINK-tum)
Christmas Cheer
Vigorous plant mounds 6" (15cm), spreads with short branching stems. Blunt green leaves turn coppery red in bright light. Easy to grow.

Senecio crassissimus

Senecio mikanioides

Senecio rowleyanus

Senecio macroglossus 'Variegatus'

Senecio ×hybridus

S. sarmentosum (sar-men-TOH-sum)
Green Carpet
Red-brown trailing stems bear tiny green leaves.

SENECIO (se-NEK-ee-oh)   **CA/WA - MS/PD**
Fast-growing, succulent foliage vines and flowering plants. Vining forms will grow in plain water. Plant in well-draining general indoor mix. Propagate vines from cuttings, flowering form from seed.
MAINTENANCE Let soil dry more between waterings when growth slows. Fertilize vines at half recommended strength every 4-8 weeks spring through fall. Leach regularly to avoid damaging accumulation of soluble salts. Trim to shape, control size, encourage bushiness and new growth. Best with relative humidity 30% or more. Check vines for mealybugs, aphids.

S. ×hybridus (HYB-ri-dus)   **ML - CA**
(*Pericallis ×hybrida*)
Cineraria
Profuse, bright flowers top 12-15" (30-38cm) plants for seasonal displays. Big leaves die back rapidly after flowers fade. Tender perennial grown from seed in cool greenhouse conditions, usually discarded after flowering. Sow seed from summer to fall for late winter, spring flowers. Transplant when small to final pots. Fertilize growing plants

at half recommended strength every 2-3 weeks. Check for powdery mildew, whitefly, aphids, leaf miners, spider mites.

S. crassissimus (kra-SIS-i-mus)
Vertical Leaf
Purple-edged 2" (5cm) leaves are held in vertical ranks on stems that grow 12-24" (30-60cm) tall.

***S. macroglossus* 'Variegatus'** (mak-roh-GLOS-us)   **ML**
Variegated Wax Vine
Spreading, trailing vine with waxy green and cream ivy-like foliage. Branches prolifically. Good basket plant.

S. mikanioides (mi-kah-nee-OI-deez)   **ML**
[*Delairea odorata* (de-LAIR-i-a oh-do-RAH-ta)]
Water Ivy, German Ivy, Parlor Ivy
Fresh green ivy-shaped leaves on fleshy, trailing stems. Fragrant yellow flowers in spring, summer. Good basket plant.

S. rowleyanus (roh-lee-AH-nus)   **BL - WA - PD/DS**
String-of-beads
Trailing succulent, basket plant has bright green bead-like leaves on slim stems that hang about 24" (60cm) long. Small, white, fragrant blossoms.

Setcreasea pallida

Sinningia 'Doll Baby'

Sinningia speciosa

Sinningia speciosa

Sinningia speciosa

Sinningia speciosa

SETCREASEA (set-KREE-see-a) BL - WA - DS
S. pallida (PAL-i-da)
[*S. purpurea, Tradescantia pallida* (tra-des-KAN-shi-a)]
Purple Heart
Strong trailing foliage plant with fleshy stems, mounding 6-12" (15-30cm) high, trailing 24-36" (60-90cm). Purple color develops in sun and strong light. Leaves grow about 6" (15cm) long. Inconspicuous small pink flowers. Easy, colorful basket plant; contrast, ground cover in plant groups. Hardy in south. Rapid growth. Plant in well-draining general indoor mix; repot as needed in late winter. Propagate from stem cuttings.
MAINTENANCE Fertilize at half recommended strength every 4-8 weeks. Trim straggly shoots, pruning longer stems right back to encourage new growth. Check for scale insects.

SINNINGIA (si-NIN-gi-a) BL - WA - H - PD
Flowering gesneriads with big, trumpet-shaped blossoms and long, velvety leaves. Many named cultivars. Colors vary from shades of purple, blue, red, pink, and white to variations with freckled throats or white edges. Woody tubers and shallow fibrous roots. Grow in humusy gesneriad mix. Repot dry tubers after dormancy; position with smooth side down and crown at soil surface. Propagate from seed, leaf cuttings, growing buds, and budded sections of dormant tubers.

S. concinna cultivars (kon-SIN-a) and
S. pusilla cultivars (poo-SIL-a)
Miniature sinningias grow and flower all year with sufficient light and humidity at 68°F (18°C) or higher. Good terrarium plants. Height and spread rarely exceed 2" (5cm).

S. speciosa cultivars (spee-si-OH-sa)
Gloxinia
Big trumpet blossoms and long velvety leaves. Specimen plants to 24-30" (60-75cm) or more across. Tolerates drier air though best with higher relative humidity.

AFTER FLOWERING, reduce watering frequency as leaves die down; stop fertilizing. When all leaves have faded, let tuber rest with dry soil in darkness at about 55°F (13°C). Repot when new growth begins; water sparingly until first leaf has expanded, then resume fertilizer applications. Tubers flower in about 3 months.
MAINTENANCE Best development in bright indirect light and day minimum of 65°F (18°C). Fertilize at half recommended strength every 3-6 weeks while growing. Trim off damaged and dying flowers and foliage. Keep crown dry to avoid crown rot. Check for whitefly, aphids, mealybugs.

Solanum pseudo-capsicum

Soleirolia soleirolii

Spathiphyllum floribundum 'Mauna Loa' (next page)

SOLANUM (so-LAH-num)   **BL - CA - MS/PD**
S. pseudo-capsicum (SOO-doh-KAP-si-kum)
Christmas, Cleveland, Jerusalem Cherry
Evergreen shrub bears attractive, inedible fruits that ripen from green to yellow and orange-red over several months in winter. Use indoors for seasonal display. Slow growth rate. Plant in well-draining general indoor mix. Propagate from seed.
Note: fruits may harm some individuals and should not be eaten.

AFTER FRUITING, let soil dry more between waterings as leaves are shed. Cut 2-3" from stems to control size and shape. Maintain dormant plant with nearly dry soil mid-late winter. Then repot to renew soil as needed. Water thoroughly and place in bright cool room or plunge pot in ground outdoors with partial shade. Fertilize actively growing plant every 4-6 weeks. Pinch shoots to shape plant until buds form. White flowers open in summer. Maintain regular watering and fertilization through fruit set and development.
MAINTENANCE Keep soil moist but not soggy while growing. Fertilizer not needed once most fruit have grown. Best with relative humidity 30% or more. Premature fruit, leaf drop result from low light, dry or wet soil. Check for other garden pests when bringing plants from outdoors, and indoors for aphids, spider mites.

SOLEIROLIA (so-lay-ROH-lee-a)   **ML - CA - H - MS/PD**
[*Helxine* (hel-ZEE-nee)]
S. solierolii (so-lay-ROH-lee-y)
Baby's-tears, Angel's-tears, Irish Moss, Japanese Moss, Corsican Carpet Plant, Mind-your-own-business, Peace-in-the-home
Small-leaved creeper for humid location. Dense mat mounds 2-4" (5-10cm). Slender, trailing stems. Tiny greenish flowers form with sufficient light. Use in dish garden, terrarium, small hanging container; as ground cover in group plantings; outdoors in warm-temperate climates. Shallow, delicate roots. Plant in shallow half-pot or dish with general indoor mix. Propagate by division and from stem cuttings that will root in water.
MAINTENANCE Avoid direct scorching sun. Let just soil surface dry between waterings. Trim to shape and to encourage bushiness. Fertilize at half recommended strength every 6-8 weeks. Leach regularly to avoid damaging accumulation of soluble salts. Brown leaf tips indicate dry air. Inadequate moisture, humidity, result in wilting and death. Chilling temperatures result in dormancy, from which baby's tears can recover. Check for spider mites.

Spathiphyllum cannifolium

Spathiphyllum wallisii

Spathiphyllum floribundum

Strelitzia reginae

SPATHIPHYLLUM (spa-thi-FIL-um)   LL/ML - WA - MS
Peace Lily, Spathe Flower

Durable, tropical foliage plants with white blossoms. Mid- to dark green, leathery leaf clusters spread slowly, become more open with age especially in low light. Each white, oval bract (spathe) reveals true flowers packed tightly on spike (spadix). Flowers best in bright indirect light. Many named cultivars with different heights, leaf and flower sizes. Easy to grow. Container or planter accent; mass for effect, line for border, edging; interiorscape plants. Tolerate low humidity, low light. Grow in well-draining humusy indoor mix; add coarser humus like fir bark or chopped osmunda fibers in larger containers. Repot as needed in spring. Propagate from seed or by division of rhizomes. Reported effective in tests to freshen or purify air (page 4).

MAINTENANCE Avoid direct hot sun. Keep soil moist during growth, flowering; let soil dry more between waterings when growth is slow. Trim faded flowers, yellowing leaves. To clean, wash with plain tepid water or clean leaves with damp soft cloth. Fertilize at half recommended strength every 1-2 months when growing. Prefers relative humidity 30% or more. Fluorides in soil and/or water may cause leaflet margin damage.

S. 'Petite' ['Bennett']: small plant grows to about 6" (15cm).

S. 'Tasson': deep green leaves; flowers readily; about 24" (60cm) tall.

S. 'Viscount': narrow glossy leaves grow to less than 12" (30cm) below abundant small white flower bracts.

Additional cultivars: **'Deneve', 'Kathlynn', 'Lillian', 'Lynise', 'Starlight'.**

S. cannifolium
Unusual foliage and flowering plant has ribbed, black-green leaves with paler undersides. White to greenish flower bracts are about 8" (20cm) long.

S. floribundum cultivars (floh-ri-BUN-dum)
Snowflower
'Mauna Loa': compact and bushy, about 24" (60cm) tall; fragrant flowers have bracts about 5" (13cm) long; needs bright light for flowering.
'Mauna Loa Supreme': tall and upright.

S. wallisii and hybrids (waw-LIS-ee-y)
Dark green leaves, height about 20" (50cm).
'Clevelandii': glossy narrow leaves and white to greenish flower bracts; drooping leaves, habit somewhat open.

Streptocarpus X hybridus

Streptocarpus X hybridus

Streptocarpus X hybridus

Streptocarpus X hybridus

Streptocarpus X hybridus

Streptocarpus saxorum

STRELITZIA (stre-LIT-zi-a) ML/BL - WA - H - PD/DS
S. reginae (re-GEE-nay)
Bird-of-Paradise Flower, Queen's Bird-of-Paradise, Crane Lily
Tropical evergreen performs best with humid warmth. Deep blue-green, 18 x 6" (45 x 15cm) leaves form vertical cluster topped by unusual bird-shaped flowers. Height 2-5' (0.6-1.5m). Needs space to develop. Specimen or group, best in greenhouse-like climate of poolside, tropical interiorscape. Tolerates lower humidity without direct hot sun. Slow growing. Plant in well-draining general or humusy indoor mix; add coarser humus like fir bark or chopped osmunda fibers in larger containers. Repot when rootbound. Propagate from seed or by division of rhizome.
MAINTENANCE Let soil dry more between waterings when growth is slow. Trim damaged, yellowing leaves, dead flowers. Clean with plain water. Fertilize every 3 months spring-fall. Avoid cold drafts.

STREPTOCARPUS (strep-toh-KAR-pus) BL - CA - H - PD
Cape Primrose
Dainty-flowered gesneriads for average temperatures. Tolerate drier air though best with relative humidity 50% or more. Shallow, fibrous roots. Plant in basic gesneriad mix. Propagate by division, from leaf cuttings, seed.
MAINTENANCE Best grown in bright indirect light, full sun in win-

ter, and temperatures of 55-75°F (13-24°C). Apply high phosphate fertilizer at half recommended strength every 4-8 weeks. Leach regularly to avoid salts damage to sensitive roots. Trim off dead and damaged flowers and leaves. Keep roots cool during hot weather by double potting: that is, enclose pot in larger container with damp (not wet) sphagnum or peat moss between the two. Spread damp moss as mulch over soil surface. Plants become dormant at low temperatures; reduce watering to match growth and do not fertilize while dormant. Check for spider mites, aphids, whitefly, and mealybugs.

S. X*hybridus* cultivars (HYB-ri-dus)
Cape Primrose
Many named cultivars offer range of colors. Strap-like, puckered leaves spread 12-18" (30-45cm) and more. Growth and flowering continues all year in well-lighted locations such as light gardens.
Weismoor Hybrids: broad-lobed flowers in reds and blues.

S. saxorum (sak-SOH-rum)
Dauphin Violet
Tiny, succulent-like creeping gesneriad has velvety oval leaves clustered on thickish stems. Pale lilac blossoms are borne gracefully above mounded plant. Good basket plant. Tolerates heat as well as cool temperatures.

Syngonium podophyllum 'White Butterfly'

Syngonium podophyllum 'Quay's California Gold'

Syngonium podophyllum 'Emerald Gem'

Thymus vulgaris: thyme

SYNGONIUM (sin-GOH-ni-um)　　ML - WA - PD
[*Nephthytis* (nef-THY-tis)]
S. podophyllum cultivars (poh-doh-FIL-um)
Nephthytis, Arrowhead Vine
Versatile, easily grown tropical vines with arrow-shaped, decorative foliage. Small clustering young plants; juvenile leaf form and color may change as slender trailing or climbing stems develop. Specimen or accent for table, shelf, basket; clustering forms useful in plant groups, smaller plants in dish gardens; climbs on pole, trellis to 10-15' (3-4.5m). Grows well in plain water. Fleshy roots grow from stems, withstand occasional drought. Plant in general or well-draining humusy indoor mix. Repot infrequently. Propagate from stem cuttings.

'Emerald Gem': compact cluster of quilted green leaves extends vining stems with more distinctly lobed foliage.
'Green Gold': robust clustered and trailing plant; leaves three-lobed, cream markings on dark green.
'Infra-red': intense pink deepens as clustered plant matures. Strong light minimizes vining.
'Quay's California Gold': irregular gold-yellow markings on clustering deep green leaves.

'White Butterfly': clustered leaves are silvery white over green, with dark green edges.
Additional cultivar: **'Robusta'** (roh-BUS-ta) ['Lemon Lime']

MAINTENANCE Let soil dry more between waterings in winter. Provide support for vines, or space for them to trail. Remove faded lower leaves. Prune to contain size. Clean plants with gentle spray of tepid water. Fertilize at half recommended strength every 8-10 weeks. Excess water can result in root rot.

THYMUS (TY-mus)　　BL - CA - PD
Thyme
Fragrant spreading perennial herb with small, shiny, oval leaves. Rose or lilac flowers cluster on 6-10" (15-25cm) stems. Add fresh leaves to flavor vinegar, salads. Dry leaves for seasoning meat, fish, poultry, and egg dishes, stuffings or dressings, and in soups and sauces. Fibrous roots. Grow in general indoor mix. Propagate by cuttings, division.
MAINTENANCE Trim to encourage vigorous new growth and to contain size. Fertilize at half recommended strength every 2-4 weeks when growth is vigorous; every 4-8 weeks during winter. Provide relative humidity 30% or more; leaves will shrivel in drier air.

Tillandsia argentea

Tillandsia caput-medusae

Tillandsia fasciculata

Tillandsia bulbosa

Tillandsia cyanea

Tillandsia ionantha

T. Xcitriodorus (sit-ree-o-DOH-rus)
Lemon Thyme
Tiny, lemon-flavored leaves.

T. vulgaris (vul-GAH-ris)
Common Thyme
Gray-green foliage, woody stems.

TILLANDSIA (ti-LAND-zi-a)　　　BL - WA - DS
Small air plants, including Spanish moss, capable of growing without soil. Display on bromeliad trees, hanging curling plant from hook, or use potted air plants for small accents. All thrive in well-ventilated places: air movement ensures renewed supplies of carbon dioxide, nitrogen, and moisture for plant growth. Flower clusters usually pink with violet blossoms. Grow on wood or tree fern bark, or pot in tree fern fiber or redwood bark chips. Short, fibrous roots penetrate growing medium. Propagate in spring from offsets and division.
AFTER FLOWERING, young plants, or offsets, grow at plant base. Separate when size is about one-third that of parent; pot or mount.
MAINTENANCE Mist air plants frequently with distilled or pure water. Fertilize at one-quarter recommended strength, spray every 4 weeks. Provide relative humidity 30% or more, especially at night. Bright bathrooms and kitchens offer ideal indoor conditions with fluctuating humidity. Check for scale insects, mealybugs, and basal rot.

T. argentea (ar-JEN-tee-a)
[*T. fucsii* (FEWK-zee-y)]
Silver Pincushion
Short gray leaves in dense, compact rosette that resembles pincushion. Thick or thin leaves. Pink flowers on slender, wiry stem.

T. balbisiana (bal-bi-zee-AH-na)
Reflexed Wild Pine
Long curving leaves spread from bulbous base. Compact in full sun, larger and greener in shade.

T. bulbosa (bul-BOH-sa)
Dancing Bulb
Bulbous base and long slender leaves that reach out like arms. Green color tints red in bright light.

T. caput-medusae (KA-put—me-DOO-zee)
Medusa's Head
Snake-like grayish green leaves curl around bulbous base. Flower cluster has red bracts and blue flowers.

T. concolor (KON-ko-lor)
Clustering, short-leaved rosette of gray leaves. Broad spike of bright red flowers.

(More *Tillandsia* species on next page)

Tillandsia punctulata

Tillandsia stricta

Tillandsia tricolor

Tillandsia streptophylla

Tillandsia tectorum

Tillandsia xerographica

Tillandsia (cont.)

T. cyanea (sy-AH-nee-a)
Pink Quill
Broad pink flower cluster with large blue-violet flowers. Color holds 2-3 months. Slender, arching, green leaves turn reddish in bright light. Adapts well to pot culture, using porous, slightly acid bromeliad mix.

T. fasciculata (fa-si-kew-LAH-ta)
Stiff-leaved Wild Pine
Large air plant has gray leaves and boldly branched flower cluster. Adapts well to pot culture.

T. grandis (GRAN-dis)
[*T. viridiflora* (vi-ri-di-FLOH-ra)]
Big, slow-growing rosette of dark blue-green, 24-36" (60-90cm), strap-shaped leaves. Adaptable: tolerates moderate light and pot culture. No offshoots; rarely flowers in cultivation.

T. ionantha (y-oh-NAN-tha)
Blushing Bride
Gray leaves blush red at flowering time. May adapt to open terrarium.

T. punctulata (punk-tew-LAH-ta)   **ML - CA**
Fairy Queen
Graceful, narrow leaves with bulbous, cup-like bases. Put water in leaf bases. Adapts to pot culture.

T. streptophylla (strep-toh-FIL-a)
Curly Locks
Twisted broad leaves and tall pink flower spike.

T. stricta (STRIK-ta)
Hanging Torch
Small gray-leaved rosette with oversized, pendulous flower cluster. Red bracts surround blue flowers.

T. tectorum (tek-TOH-rum)
Dense rosettes of fuzzy leaves surround pink flower clusters.

T. tricolor (TRY-ku-lor)
Tri-colored Air Plant
Dense rosette of narrow, gray-green leaves. Red flowering spike bears violet blossoms. Tolerates moderate light.

T. xerographica (zee-roh-GRAF-i-ka)
Broad silvery leaves curl back to form ball-shaped rosette. Prefers full sun. Yellow-pink flowering stem with bluish flowers.

Tradescantia fluminensis 'Variegata'

Tolmiea menziesii

Tradescantia fluminensis

Tradescantia fluminensis 'Albovittata'

TOLMIEA (tol-MEE-a)   BL - CA - PD
T. menziesii (men-ZEE-zee-y)
Piggyback Plant, Mother-of-thousands

Temperate, native foliage plant for cool, humid position. Big fresh green maple-shaped leaves on long stems form widespreading, trailing rosette. Height 6-8" (15-20cm), spread 12-24" (30-60cm) and more. New plant develops at base of every leaf-blade. Easy to grow specimen or accent for table, basket. Tolerates short periods at 40°F (5°C). Grow in well-draining general indoor mix. Repot or replace plant each year. Propagate from plantlets that root easily on soil or in plain water.
MAINTENANCE Avoid direct, scorching sun. Trim, removing older leaves to contain size and encourage new growth. Fertilize at half recommended strength every 4-8 weeks spring-summer. Leach regularly to avoid damaging accumulation of soluble salts. Best with relative humidity 30% or more. Thin, spindly growth in low light. Check for spider mites, aphids, mealybugs.

TEMPERATURE (page 7)
  CA - COOL to AVERAGE TEMPERATURES: days 60-75°F (16-24°C), nights as cool as 45°F (7°C).
  WA - AVERAGE to WARM TEMPERATURES: days 70-80°F (21-27°C), nights 60-65°F (16-18°C).

TRADESCANTIA (tra-des-KAN-shi-a)   ML/BL - CA - PD
T. fluminensis (floo-mi-NEN-sis)
[*T. albiflora* (al-bi-FLOH-ra)]
Spiderwort, Wandering Jew, Speedy Henry

Trailing foliage plants with slender fleshy stems. Green foliage, green or purplish undersides. Cultivars variable, with stripes and segmented variegations. Leaf length 1½-3" (4-7.5cm). Tiny white flowers. Easy to grow. Small table accents, larger specimens for baskets; useful contrasts in plant group; grow well in plain water. Rapid growth. Slender, shallow roots. Plant in well-draining general indoor mix; repot or renew as needed. Propagate from stem cuttings.

'Albovittata': green and white striped foliage.
'Variegata': creamy stripes, segments, and whole leaves.

MAINTENANCE Avoid direct sun. Best with nights above 50°F (10°C). Trim to encourage bushiness, prune older shoots in favor of new growth. Fertilize at half recommended strength every 4-8 weeks. Leach regularly to avoid damaging accumulation of soluble salts. Weak, spindly growth in low light. Variegated forms develop best color in bright indirect light; trim out plain green shoots. Check for mealybugs, scale insects.

Tulipa

Vanda

Tulipa

Vanda

TULIPA (TEW-li-pa)   ML/BL - CA - MS/PD
Tulip

Spring bulb flowers for seasonal indoor decoration. Colorful, single or double blossoms with sturdy blue-green foliage. Accent or massed for larger-scale effect. Plant mature bulbs in pots or bowls, close together but not touching each other or container. For uniform foliage orientation, face bulbs' flat sides outwards. Use humusy indoor mix, with bulb tips at or just above soil surface. Water thoroughly. Maintain in dark, cool (40-50°F, 5-10°C) place for 10-12 weeks until roots are well-developed and shoot tips start to grow. Add water if soil dries out during this time. After cool period, provide light so leaves can turn green. Move tulips to living area when flower buds swell. Water to keep soil moist but not soggy.

AFTER FLOWERING, continue regular watering while leaves are green. Plant outdoors in spring; let foliage die back naturally. Varieties that were forced commercially for early flowering may not flower next spring, but healthy leaves revitalize bulbs for coming season.

> **WATERING** (page 8)
> **MS** - Keep soil moist.
> **PD** - Let soil become partly dry between waterings.
> **DS** - Allow soil to dry out between thorough waterings.

VANDA (VAN-da)   ML - WA - H - PD
Moon Orchid, Vanda Orchid

Tropical orchids for airy yet humid climates. Long-lasting, glossy, usually fragrant 2-3" (5-10cm) blossoms grow in clusters from leaf axils. Epiphytic: mount to hang in humid greenhouse climate. Indoors, plant in well-draining, moisture retaining mix containing both fibrous and water-holding materials: osmunda, coarsely shredded fir bark, redwood chips, or small pumice stones, with coarse peat moss and/or perlite. Or use ready-made epiphytic orchid mix. Reduce depth of growing medium with deep underlayer of clean broken pot. Support rooting, branched stem on bark strip. Fleshy roots with pale outer layer. Repot in spring every few years to renew soil. Propagate from stem cuttings, using rooting lateral branches.

MAINTENANCE Prefer brighter light in late fall and winter. Best with nights above 50°F (10°C). Let soil dry more between waterings in winter when plant grows more slowly. Fertilize every 2-4 weeks spring through summer, every 4-8 weeks in fall and winter. Or spray with dilute fertilizer solution every 1-2 weeks when growth is rapid. Root rot results from poor drainage, overwatering. Dark leaves and soft new growth result from insufficient light. Check for slugs and snails on orchids moved in from shade outdoors, and for spider mites, scale insects, mealybugs, rots, and leafspot on those indoors.

Vriesea 'Mariae'

Vriesea gigantea

Vriesea pulmonata

Vriesea 'Rex'

Vriesea fosteriana 'Red Chestnut'

Vriesea splendens 'Major'

VRIESEA (VREE-see-a) ML/LL - WA - MS

Elegantly symmetrical bromeliad with various leaf colors. Flattened flower cluster often brightly colored, lasts several months. Accent, specimen, or group. Tolerates shade. Small, fleshy root system; established plants rarely need repotting. Grow in porous, slightly acid bromeliad mix. Propagate in spring from offsets.

AFTER FLOWERING, young plants or offsets grow at plant base. When one-third the size of parent plant, cut at base and pot .

MAINTENANCE Keep water in central cup at all times. In winter, let soil dry out for short periods. Clean upper leaf surfaces gently with moist soft cloth. Fertilize at one-quarter recommended strength, applied to soil and cup every 4 weeks. Provide relative humidity 30% or more; brown leaf tips indicate dry air. Trim damaged, discolored parts. Check for scale insects; avoid use of oil sprays that damage food-absorbing tissues.

V. 'Mariae' [V. ✕mariae], **Painted Feather:** gleaming red and yellowish-green flower cluster. Best in humid climate.

V. 'Rex' : red and yellow flower stalk rises from dark green leafy rosette.

V. 'Splendide': silvery cross-bands on arched leaves; slender branched flower cluster.

V. fosteriana 'Red Chestnut' (fos-te-ree-AH-na)
Dark leaves have pale green flecks and bands. Elegant 1-2' (20-60 cm) rosette flushes maroon in diffused bright light. Best in humid climate.

V. gigantea (jy-GAN-tee-a)
Big, bold funnel rosette of flat green leaves grows 6-7' (1.8-2.1m) high, spreads to about 5' (1.5m). Red bracts on branched flowering stem.

V. pulmonata (pul-mo-NAH-ta)
Red, branching flower cluster rises above clear green foliage.

V. splendens cultivars (SPLEN-denz)
Flaming Sword
Broad green leaves with brown crossbands. Flower cluster of red bracts, yellow blossoms, rises 24-30" (60-90cm) above formal leafy rosette.
'Major' [V. splendens var. major]: large form, more colorful.
'Favorite': narrow, red-orange flower stem.

YUCCA (YOO-ka, YUK-a) BL/ML - WA - DS
Y. elephantipes (e-le-fan-TEE-payz)
[Y. gigantea (jy-gan-TEE-a)]
Spineless Yucca
Durable plant has cluster of leathery leaves on woody stems. Height to 5' (1.5m) or more. Needs space. Easy to grow. Tolerates periods of low light and cooler temperatures. Rarely flowers indoors. Plant in sandy indoor mix; repot rarely. Propagate from offsets (suckers) and stem cuttings.

(Continued on next page)

Yucca elephantipes

Zamia pumila

Zebrina pendula

Yucca elephantipes (cont'd.)
'Variegata', Giant Variegated Palm-lily: leaves have ivory border.
MAINTENANCE Let soil dry out more between waterings in winter.
Wash with plain water to clean. Fertilize at half recommended strength
every 8-12 weeks. Leach regularly to avoid damaging accumulation
of soluble salts. Fluorides in soil and/or water cause some leaflet margin damage. Check for scale insects, root mealybugs.

ZAMIA (ZAH-mi-a)   **BL/ML - CA - PD**
Z. pumila (PEW-mi-la)
[*Z. furfuracea* (fur-few-RAH-see-a)]
Florida Arrowroot, Sago Cycas, Cardboard Palm
Cycad has sturdy short trunk below stiffly spreading palm-like leaves.
Broad, leathery, metallic green leaflets, brown dusty undersides and
stems. Compact, very slow growth. Mature height 4-6' (1.2-1.8m).
Tolerates lower temperatures. Avoid hot, dry, unmoving air. Repot as
needed in well-draining general indoor mix with added humus.
MAINTENANCE In winter, let soil become partly dry between water-
ings. Wipe with damp soft cloth to remove dust. Fertilize every 2-3
months spring through fall. Trim damaged and discolored foliage.
Check for scale insects.

ZEBRINA (zee-BRY-na)   **ML/BL - CA - PD**
Z. pendula (PEN-dew-la)
[*Tradescantia zebrina* (tra-des-KAN-shi-a)]
Wandering Jew
Trailing foliage plants with slender fleshy stems. Dark green 2" (5cm)
foliage with broad silver bands, purple undersides. Tiny pink flowers.
Small table accents, larger specimens for baskets; useful contrast in
plant group. Grow well in plain water. Rapid growth. Slender, shallow
roots. Plant in well-draining general indoor mix; repot or renew as
needed. Propagate from stem cuttings. Several named cultivars.

'Purpusii' [*Z. purpusii*], **Bronze Wandering Jew:** dark red or reddish
green foliage.

'Quadricolor' : gleaming leaves with stripes of green, red, white.

MAINTENANCE Avoid direct sun. Best with nights above 50°F (10°C).
Trim to encourage bushiness, prune out older shoots. Fertilize at half
recommended strength every 4-8 weeks. Leach regularly to avoid damaging accumulation of soluble salts. Best with relative humidity 30%
or more. Weak, spindly growth in low light. Variegated forms develop
best color in bright indirect light. Check for mealybugs, scale insects.

INDEX

INDEX (cont'd)

INDEX (cont'd)